JOKES FOR ALL OCCASIONS

JOKES
FOR ALL OCCASIONS

Compiled by
Dr. P.S. Sood

HIND POCKET BOOKS

JOKES FOR ALL OCCASIONS
© Hind Pocket Books, 1996
First Edition: 1995
Sixth Reprint: 1996
Seventh Reprint: 1997
Eighth Reprint: 2002
Nineth Reprint: March 2005
ISBN 81-216-0067-7

Published by **Hind Pocket Books (P) Ltd.**
J-40, Jorbagh Lane, New Delhi-110003
Tel: 24620063, 55654197 • Fax: 24645795
E-mail: fullcircle@vsnl.com

Typesetting: SCANSET

J-40, Jorbagh Lane, New Delhi-110003
Tel: 24620063, 55654197 • Fax: 24645795

Printed at Nice Printing Press, Delhi-110051

PRINTED IN INDIA
96/05/09/03/21/SCANSET/SAP/NPP/KE

A humorist must not live too far from the ground nor too close. He must post himself on a small hill, high enough to see things with the necessary detachment, but not so high as to lose sight of them.

— *Giovanni Mosca*

Act/Aim
i.e. Advise and Advertise

One city window-cleaning firm in England advertises itself as TRANSPARENT WALL MAINTEN-ANCE ENGINEERS.

* *

The two thieves had just got home after robbing a big bank.

"Let's see how much we got!" said the first.

"No, I'm tired," said the second. "We'll find out from the morning papers."

ob: "I thought I asked you to come after supper!"
o : "That's what I came after."

* *

"Do you have an opening for an enterprising young man?" the earnest job-seeker asked the potential employer.
"Yes, I do," the latter replied tartly, "and close it ently as you go out."

* *

A clergyman, who had advertised for an organist, received this reply:
"I notice you have a vacancy for an organist and music teacher, either lady or gentleman.. Having been both for several years, I beg to apply for the position."

* *

Pat: "Have any of your childhood hopes been realised?"
Mat: "Yes. When mother used to comb my hair, I wished I didn't have any."

* *

"Are you sure this cure of yours for baldness is really effective?" asked a customer.
"Not just effective, it's extraordinary! Just think, a customer of ours, who was as bald as an egg, began our cure and, twenty days later, when he received our bill he was already able to tear his hair!"

* *

Seen on the menu outside a restaurant in London:
"Between 4 and 7 p.m., tea and snakes will be served."

8

Jacques Charon, director-star of the Comedie Francaise, was trying to get a young actor to show more ardour while kissing the heroine. "Look", Charon said. "Imagine it's 5 p.m. and her husband is due home in two minutes. Imagine at the same time that you want to see her tomorrow. Now give her a good-bye kiss..."

* *

Advice to office girls: "Take your shorthand at arm's length."

* *

Following a knock on the door of an undergraduate's room at a university, a voice asked: "May I come in? This is the room I had when I was at college." He was invited in.

"Yes." he went on musingly: "Same old room. Same old furniture. Same old view from the window. Same old closet."

He opened the closet-door. There stood a girl, looking scared.

"That's my sister," said the occupant of the room.

"Yes," replied the visitor. "Same old story."

* *

"What am I supposed to do with this?" grumbled the motorist as the police clerk handed him a receipt for his traffic fine.

"Keep it," the clerk advised. "When you get four of them, you get a bicycle."

"My poor man," said the kind old lady to the beggar, "it must be dreadful to be lame. But think how much worse it would be if you were blind!"

"You're right, lady," agreed the beggar. "When I was blind, I was always getting counterfeit money!"

* *

Abstract art is that which uses a variety of means to express nothing.

* *

Dad: "If you're good, I'll give you a shiny new penny."

Lad: "How about a dirty old nickel?"

* *

A Rio de Janeiro insurance company has done some investigation to establish the most dangerous occupation in Brazil. The statistics it has studied reveal the ones to suffer most from physical violence are the football referees. Next come marriage brokers.

* *

Nearly every film actor, writer and director has an agent, whose 10 per cent fee is a fact of life as inevitable as death and taxes. Consider the writer who was giving blood to the Red Cross. As the blood flowed into the tube, he exclaimed: "Don't fill it all the way up! Ten per cent belongs to my agent."

* *

"So, young man, you want to become my son-in-law?"

"Not exactly, sir, but, if I marry your daughter, I don't see how I can avoid it."

10

Rehearsal: Show at which the main role is played by the director.

* *

One plunging neckline to another: "Don't dance with the General—his medals are cold."

* *

The irate psychiatrist had just about enough arguing with his stubborn patient. ' I'm warning you, Balu," he snapped finally. "If you don't pay my bill, I'll let you go crazy!"

* *

A modern employer is one who is looking for men between the ages of 25 and 30 with 40 years' experience.

* *

Employer: "For this job we want a responsible man."
Applicant: "That's me. Wherever I've worked, if anything went wrong, they said I was responsible."

* *

"I want some shirts for my husband," she said, "but I am afraid I have forgotton the collar size."
"Thirteen and a half, Ma'am?" suggested the shop assistant.
"That's it! How did you know?"
"Men who let their wives buy their shirts for them are always about that size, Ma'am," explained the observant salesman.

* *

"My boy," said the magnate to his son, "there are two things that are vitally necessary if you are to succeed in business."
"What are they, Dad?"
"Honesty and sagacity."

"What's honesty?"

"Always—no matter what happens or how adversely it may affect you—always keep your word once you've given it."

"And sagacity?"

"Never give it."

* *

"Making lifesize enlargements of snapshots is our speciality," announced the shop assistant to the customer.

"Fine," said the customer, handing him a tiny photograph.

"Here's a picture I took of Mount Everest."

* *

Never kick a man when he is down—he may get up.

* *

Some little kids out in Actors' Colony decided to play House. "I'll be the Mama," said one little girl. "I'll be the Papa," one boy volunteered.

The third child piped in with: "I'll be the divorce lawyer."

* *

"My sister does fancy work."

"And what do you do?"

"Oh, I don't fancy work."

* *

In the application form for a new driver's licence one question was, "Have you ever been arrested?" The applicant put down. "No". The next question was, "Why?" The applicant put down, "Never been caught."

12

"Father," said a small boy, "What is a demagogue?"
"A demagogue, my son, is a man who can force the boat himself and persuade everybody else that there is a terrible storm at sea."

* *

When landlords in the Los Angeles area advertise their residences for sale, they generally mention the availability of tennis. Newspapers carry ads for homes with a tennis court, homes that include a tennis-club membership, and some that suggest "room for tennis court".
But a recent ad in "The Los Angeles Times" contained a new twist. "Almost tennis-court-size backyard," it read.

* *

British guide (showing places of interest): "It was in this room that Lord Wellington received his first Commission."
American tourist (suddenly interested): "How much was it?"

* *

On the menu card of a snack bar at Dadar, Bombay: "FOR SUGGESTIONS PLEASE THE MANAGER".

* *

A monument to grandmothers will be erected in Belgrade. Authorities have approved a suggestion by representatives of a residential district in the Yugoslav capital that gratitude be shown in this way 'for extraordinary merit in the education and care of grandchildren'. The monument will stand in one of the Belgrade parks where grandmothers keep busy looking after the little ones.

13

Traffic sign: "DO NOT PARK VERTICAL."

* *

"Isn't Rs. 110 a little high for a sweater?" the customer asked.

"Not really, madame. It's all wool, shorn from a very special breed of sheep whose habitat is the most inaccessible region of the Himalayan Mountains," explained the clerk. "It is truly a beautiful yarn."

"Yes," said the customer, "and you tell it well, too."

* *

A sign near a lift manages to deal with the two prominent problems: "To conserve our energy and to promote your health, please use our stairs for short trips."

* *

A farmer concerned about well-meaning holiday makers feeding his horse, pinned a notice to his fence: "Please do not feed cakes and buns to the horse. Signed: The Owner."

Shortly afterwards, another notice appeared below the first. It read: "Please pay no attention to the above notice. Signed: The Horse."

* *

Advertisement for disposable feeding bottles: "Hurry up and have a baby while this offer lasts."

One day while I was on my way to work, our bus driver suddenly pulled to a stop, opened the door and jumped out. It crossed my mind that he was probably getting his morning coffee—on my time. Then, to my amazement, I saw him help a young blind woman across two busy streets. I am sure that, as he boarded the bus again, I was not the only one there who felt like clapping.

* *

Headline to an article in "The New York Daily News" about the capture of a horse running loose through a Brooklyn park: "NABBED FOR ILLEGAL GAMBOLLING."

* *

On an article in "The Star" about an Austin Texas, a man who claims to be the world's speediest talker: "FASTEST GUMS IN TOWN".

* *

From a report by Prentice-Hall, the research and publishing firm, on an agreement giving male employees of the US Labour Department time off when their children are born: "MEN IN LABOUR GET PATERNITY LEAVE."

* *

On a New York magazine account about reduced travel rates: "THE FAIREST OF THE FARES."

* *

Going around an exhibition of paintings done by a friend of ours, a portrait caught my attention. It was titled "My Husband" and below it was written, "Not for sale".

I had just entered our local sub-post office with my small dog firmly attached to a lead when I noticed a "Dogs Not Allowed" notice boldly displayed on the door. Turning to the postmistress, I apoligized for bringing my dog.

"I don't mind the ones on leads with their owners," she replied. "The notice is for those big dogs who come in on their own."

* *

Sign at entrance to a nurses' mess near the Indo-Pak border: "No Man's Land."

* *

Social note in "Canadian Reader": "Nigel Napier-Andrews was married recently. Mr. Napier-Andrews is the author of *How to Eat Well and Stay Single.*"

* *

Sign in the window of a New York Furriers : "Sale starts Friday 9 a.m. Furs come, furs served."

* *

Pretty secretary hurrying out of office of greying executive: "What they say about Mr. Wilton is true. He's in his second wolfhood."

* *

Sign in a jewellery-store window: "We're the ring leaders."

* *

An artist who was spending a vacation in an out-of the-way town entered the general store and asked if they had camel's hairbrushes.

"No, sir," replied the store owner. "You see, we never had to call for them. Nobody in these parts is known to keep camels."

16

A merchant took out a fire insurance policy and, the same day, his store was burned to the ground. The insurance company suspected fraud but couldn't prove anything. It had to content itself with writing the following letter:

"Dear Sir: You took out an insurance policy at 10 a.m. and your fire did not break out until 3.30 p.m. Will you kindly explain the delay?"

* *

"Darling, why are you making faces at the bull-dog?" asked the mother of a three-year-old anxiously.

Her little son replied indignantly: "Well, the dog started it."

* *

In a factory, a newly recruited Labour and Welfare Officer placed a signboard near the entrance which read: IN CASE OF FIRE, FLEE THE BUILDING WITH THE SAME SPEED THAT IS SHOWN AT QUITTING TIME.

* *

Solly Goldberg was making sure he would win the Best Salesman award. Not only did he sell a milking machine to an Arab farmer who only had one cow, he took the cow as a deposit.

* *

The first man to make a mountain out of a molehill was probably a real estate agent.

* *

Weary salesclerk: "Did you ever wonder how many fig leaves Eve tried on before she said, 'I'll take this one'?"

Shopper: "My wallet's full of big bills—and I wish some of them were paid."

* *

A clerk at the telephone board in a Bombay bookshop received an order er for *She Strips to Conquer*.

* *

High on a wall in Edinburgh, Scotland, is this official announcement: "Smoking stops you from growing." Beneath, about 60 centimetres from the ground, someone pencilled: "Now you tell me."

* *

A former director-general of the BBC was explaining the impossibility of drawing up specific codes of practice in the matter of taste. He cited the answer given by a well-meaning curate who, when asked "Where exactly do you draw the line on bosoms?" said, "It depends a good deal on the bosom."

* *

A famous actor explained what a cameo role was: "That's when your contract is longer than your script."

* *

Advertising wasn't always as aggressive as it is today. This advertisement appeared in an American newspaper 50 years ago: "The public is kindly requested to buy Universal Whitener tooth powder. It is neither better nor worse than most of the others in my store, but I think it is just about as good as any of them, and I particularly recommend it because it is made by my nephew, who is a very deserving young man and hopes to be married soon on the strength of it."

18

Woman to bookstore clerk: "What I'd really like is a 21-day diet that goes as fast as a 21-day holiday."

* *

People on holiday complain of an inability to meet other people. But Frankfurt, Germany, tourist-expert Horst Egon Scholz has come to the rescue with his campaign "Contact Button". The button carries the inscription "International Tourist," the name of the wearer, his nationality and the languages he can speak, symbolized by national flags. With this badge worn on one's lapel, it is possible to break the ice more easily when on holiday. The Contact Button was tested by travel experts during four months last year in Britain, France, Spain and Greece, and the response was overwhelming. It is now available in all Trans Europe travel agencies in West Germany.

* *

British actress Joyce Grenfell recalls that while she and her friend Viola Tunnard were on a hospital tour in India during World War II, they were invited to a service club dance at Poona. "We were made to feel irresistible—lines formed to await our favours on the dance floor," she writes. "But we were a little surprised to hear ourselves announced as 'two well-known artistes who have been flown out from home to entertain men in bed.'"

A group of clergy touring Australia was accommodated in one town in a girls' school dormitory which was uninhabited because of holidays. There they found this notice; "If you require a mistress during the night, press this bell."

* *

The trouble with the publishing business is that too many people who have half a mind to write a book do so.

* *

"Okay, you are appointed," said the executive, moving around his table towards the beautiful young stenotypist. "Now would you like to try for a raise?"

* *

Visitor: "What have you in here?"
Guide: "Remains to be seen, sir. This is the morgue."

* *

They were looking down into the depth of the Grand Canyon (U.S.A.). "Do you know," asked the guide, "that it took millions and millions of years for this great abyss to be carved out?"
"Well, well!" ejaculated the traveller.
"I never knew this was a Government job."

* *

Artist: "I'd like to donate my last picture to a charitable purpose."
Critic: "Why not give it to an institution for the blind?"

* *

"I saw your advertisement to the effect that you recover umbrellas. I'd like mine recovered."
"Yes, sir, where is it?"
"If I knew that I'd recover it myself."

20

Visitor: "Do you believe that departed people communicate with you?"
Medium: "Oh, yes, my husband sends me alimony every week."

* *

St. Peter: "How did you get here?"
New Arrival: "Flu."

* *

Mountain climber: "I can't seem to improve upon my work."
Youth: "I guess you've reached your peak."

* *

Director Alfred Hitchcock: "Suspense is a matter of knowledge. If a bomb unexpectedly goes off in a film—that's surprise. But if the audience knows a bomb will go off in five minutes, and the hero on screen doesn't know it—that's suspense!"

* *

When an actor proposed to his girl-friend, she replied, "Darling, I do love you and want to marry you. But it frightens me to hear that you've been married five times before."
"Darling!" cried the actor. "Why listen to a lot of old wives' tales?"

* *

Customer: "I inserted an advertisement for my lost dog in the paper here. Has anything been heard of it? I offered a reward of $10,000."
Office boy: "Sorry, all the editors and reporters are out looking for the dog."

The stingy salesman, while on an out-of-town sales trip, sent his wife a cheque for a million kisses as an anniversary present. The wife was quite annoyed and sent back a postcard: "Dear Dick, Thanks for the anniversary cheque. The milkman cashed it for me just this morning."

* *

Customer to used-car salesman: "What I'd really like is a car that runs as smoothly as you talk."

* *

Office manager to employee: "Don't think of me as a boss but as your friend who is always right."

* *

"Hello, hello?" shrilled a spinsterish voice over the phone.
"Is this the S.P.C.A.?"
"Yes."
"I want you to send somebody over right away."
"What's wrong?"
"There's a horrid magazine salesman sitting in a tree teasing my dog."

* *

Director: "Yes, jump now!"
Actor: "I won't make that jump! There's only two feet of water at the bottom!"
Director: "So what?" replied the director. "We don't want you to drown!"

* *

In the film studio the carpenters were making a new scenery set when the film director got annoyed. In exasperation he barked, "Hey! make noise more quietly!"

Producer: "Sorry, the director informs that your lyrics are two coloured—even for technicolour!"

Lyric writer: "What do you mean?"

Producer: "In the first few lines, the hero turns red, the heroine turns purple, the villain turns green and the vamp turns almost white."

* *

Film extra: "So, would you get my signatures on the contract, sir?"

Producer: "A verbal contract is enough!"

Film extra: "But sir, last time I'd a verbal contract and I drew a verbal salary."

* *

Film star: "If you send a good reporter, I'll give the full story of the murder."

Editor: "When did the murder take place?"

Film star: "Next Friday. You can be the witness to the whole tragedy."

* *

Director: "Cut! Cut! Cut!"

Photographer: "Hero, cut!"

Director: "I mean cut the portion where the hero speaks the dialogue."

* *

A French actress received this letter from one of the moviegoers; "I love your brownish hair, your dark black eyes, your beautiful face and lovely cheeks and reddish skirt with can can." This boy, she explains, writes descriptions of missing persons for the police.

"I'm a young actress driving to Bombay for a screen test. What shall I take along?"
"Better take a spare reputation!"

* *

Director: "Your acting in the scene was superb! Your suffering was so true, so real!"
Actress: "That is because two nails got stuck in my shoe!"
Director: "Then let them be there until we finish the scene."

* *

A movie actor's recent tour was a grand success. He outran every audience.

* *

Customer: "Why did you drop that hot towel on my face?"
Barber: "Do you think I was going to burn my fingers?"

* *

Norwegian art collector Halvorsen once asked the artist Edward Munch if he had a reliable criterion for success of a portrait. "Yes, indeed," said Munch. "If I paint a person and his enemies find the likeness true, I am satisfied. The subject himself may disagree, but I know for sure that the picture is a success."

* *

The Karnataka Government recently made it compulsory for motorcyclists to wear crash helmets and their sale shot up. Many advertisements began appearing all over the State trying to sell various makes of helmets, but the one which caught my eye read: "Prevent brain drain—Use Honda helmets."

George Bernard Shaw was sitting in the stalls when I attended a performance of his play *Androcles and the Lion* at the Festival Theatre in Cambridge. At the end of the play we called, "Author, author!" insistently until, at last, he arose. He turned to face us and said, "This play already has one lion"—and sat down.

* *

To the delight of the audience, a concert in York, England, opened with the loudspeaker announcement: "Monsieur Tortelier has lost his clothes on the plane and begs your indulgence."

* *

"The whole of Italy," said G.B. Shaw "is a theatre and all the people are actors—and the worst ones are on the stage."

* *

The popular French actress, Corinne Caluet, once remarked: "Hollywood must be the cleanest town in the world, because so many people are always washed up."

* *

Hollywood's popular actress Ava Gardner once pointed out to her cameraman: "You are not photographing my best side."
"How can I?" snapped the Cameraman. "You're always sitting on it."

* *

G.B. Shaw once entered the dressing room of an inflated matinee idol who was slowly and smugly arranging his tie, smoothing his hair and caressing his lapel before a full-length mirror.

"You know," said Shaw, "I envy you, old boy. You must be the happiest man in the world. You're in love with yourself and you don't have a rival on this planet."

* *

The friend enquired from a new actor: "Is your first picture a comedy or a tragedy?"
Actor: "If loads of tickets are sold, it's a comedy. Otherwise it is a tragedy!"

* *

Theatre manager: "The orchestra seats are three rupees, the balcony seats are two rupees and the stalls are fifty naya paisa only."
Customer: "And any ticket for sitting on the floor?"

* *

"The movies would be better if they shot less film and more actors!"

* *

Male actor: "He can't do anything wrong. He is a king here."
Female actor: "If the king can do no wrong, how does he ever have any fun?"

* *

A young playwright once prevailed on George Bernard Shaw to listen to his new play. Before the second act was over, Shaw was fast asleep. The young dramatist shook him awake, complaining he was there to give a comment on his work.
"My dear fellow," said Shaw, "you asked me for a comment on your play. Sleep is a comment."

Shopkeeper: "These are especially strong pants, Sir. They simply laugh at laundry."
Customer: "I know that kind; I had some which came back with their sides split."

* *

A lady customer entered a ready-made garments shop and sought out the salesman who had waited on her the previous day.
"You said this sweater was 100% wool," she complained. "And here I find a chit sewed inside on which is printed 'All Cotton'...."
"What are you worried about lady?" the salesman shrugged. "That ticket is only in there to scare the moths away."

* *

"You don't believe in hell?"
"No."
"Then, where has the business gone?"

* *

"Have you ever laughed until you cried?"
"Yes, just this morning I did."
"How?"
"Father stepped on a tack. I laughed, he saw me, and then I cried."

* *

Dad: "You mustn't pull the cat's tail."
Sonny: "I'm only holding it. The cat is pulling."

27

Customer (on the telephone): "Three of those apples you sent me were rotten. I am bringing them back."
Storekeeper: "That's all right, madam. You needn't bring them back. Your word is just as good as the apples."

* *

The man bought a cigar, and then left. Five minutes later he dashed back to the store.
"That cigar," he shouted, "is simply awful."
"It's all very well for you to complain," said the storekeeper. "You've only got one; I've got hundreds of the darn things."

* *

Customer: "Take a look at what you did to this!"
Laundryman: "I can't see anything wrong with that piece of lace."
Customer: "Lace, hell, that was a sheet!"

* *

"Did you hear the joke about the film star?"
"No, what is it?"
"Her secretary didn't keep the records straight and now she finds she has had two more divorces than she's had weddings."

* *

The censor: "About this picture, *Beaches and Peaches*, you call it an educational film. What does it teach?"
The movie producer: "Anatomy."

"This is my birthday, you know," said the matinee idol.

"Many happy returns," replied his friend. "How old aren't you?"

* *

Director: "Now in this scene I want you to make love to her like a bear or a gorilla or something."
Actor: "Yes, sir, I'll do the beast I can."

* *

Professor: "What does that V on your sweater stand for?"
College girl: "Virgin."
Professor: "You a virgin?"
College girl: "Well, it's an old sweater."

* *

Door-to-door salesman to housewife: "I'd like to show you a little item your neighbours said you couldn't afford."

* *

A sales clerk went to the manager with a problem. "How," he asked, "can I stop women customers from complaining about our prices and talking about the low prices in the good old days?"
"Very easily," replied the manager. "Act surprised and tell them you didn't think they were old enough to remember them."

Belle/Beau
i.e. Blonde and Boy

Girl to fireman: "It must have taken a lot of courage to rescue me as you did."

Fireman: "Yes. I had to knock down three other guys who wanted to do it."

* *

Girls were made before mirrors. And they've stayed there ever since.

* *

Two women met several years after one of them had married a man both had been in love with. "At least," said the married one cattily, "you've lost a little weight since those days. You were pretty fat..."

"Yes," said the unmarried one. "It's better to have loved and lost than to have won and gained."

Taste in women varies. Out West, they like their liquor strong and women weak. Down South, they like their liquor hard and women soft. Up North, they want their liquor straight and women curved.

* *

"Did you ever see a company of women silent?"
"Yes."
"When?"
"When the Chairperson asked the oldest lady to speak up."

* *

He: "What keeps your shoulder-strap up?"
She: "Your extreme timidity, I suppose."

* *

Shortly after her husband reported her missing, the police found Constancia Tersini living rough in a railyard near Rome. She refused to return to her husband. "We met while playing mixed doubles tennis," she said. "When we married we planned to have two boys and two girls, to form our own mixed doubles. Now my husband is bored with tennis and mad about football. There are 11 boys in a soccer team and I'm worried."

* *

Marriage begins when she sinks in your arms and you end with your arms in the sink.

* *

During his honeymoon the Scotsman took his wife to see the dentist who, after making an examination, said: "Dear, dear, these teeth ought to have been taken out years ago!"
"All right," said the Scot. "Carry on and take them out and send the bill to her father."

31

A man and his wife were studying a religious painting at an art gallery when he said: "I wonder why angels are never portrayed wearing beards."

"I suppose," came the reply from his wife, "it's because a man gets to heaven by a very close shave."

* *

"I was a fool when I married you," grumbled a wife. Her husband flashed with anger: "Well, don't blame me—I didn't know at the time."

* *

She's the kind of girl who doesn't care for a man's company—unless he owns it.

* *

The best way to approach a woman with a past is with a present.

* *

Our Research Department has come up with significant statistics that the average number of times a girl says No to temptation is once weakly.

* *

Before retiring on his wedding night, the young minister turned to his bride and murmured: "Pardon me darling, I'm going to pray for guidance."

"Sweetheart," his wife answered, "I'll take care of the guidance. You pray for endurance."

* *

A Hollywood beauty is an expert housekeeper. Every time she gets divorced, she keeps the house.

* *

"See that boy over there annoying Mary?"

"Why, he isn't even looking at her."

"Yes, that's just what's annoying her."

A man who thinks marriage is a 50-50 proposition doesn't understand either women or percentages.

* *

Women are the kind of problem most men like to wrestle with.

* *

Man's greatest labour-saving device is the love of a rich woman.

* *

"You never can tell about men," the sophisticated miss advised her younger sister. "Either they're so slow you want to scream—or so fast you have to!"

* *

Tactful husband to wife: "How do you expect me to remember your birthday when you never look any older?"

* *

It was the teenager's first visit to a perfume counter. Her eyes roved uneasily over the lurid trade names: "Night of Passion", "Mad Embrace", "Irresistible" …Finally, she mustered enough courage to appro ach the salesgirl. "Pardon me," she asked demure ly, "but do you have anything for a beginner?"

* *

The Duke of Windsor was telling a group of admirers how to keep their wives happy. "Of course," he concluded with a smile, "I do have one slight edge over the rest of you. It helps a pinch to be able to remind your bride that you gave up a throne for her."

The lads at the corner drugstore were exchanging stories about their experiences with the opposite sex.

"Aw," sniffed one, "girls are a dime a dozen."

"Gee!" sighed a younger lad who had remained silent until then. "And all this time I've been buying jelly beans."

* *

Two young women were discussing how tall they would like to be.

"Five-foot-six would be perfect," said one.

"Yes," said her friend. "But, if you were five foot three, you'd have three more inches of boys to choose from."

* *

A sexy blonde with a stunning figure boarded a bus and, finding no vacant seats, asked a gentleman for his, explaining she was expecting. The man stood up at once and gave her his seat but couldn't help commenting she didn't look it.

"Well," she replied with a smile, "it's only been about half an hour."

* *

"May I see some mirrors, please?" asked the lady shopper.

"Hand-mirrors, Madam?" queried the assistant.

"No," said the lady, "ones you can see your face in."

* *

A sexy movie star was feeling sick. She went to her doctor—and he advised her to stay "out of bed" for a week.

Billie: "Was your marriage one of those trial-and-error things?"
Willie: "Just the opposite! First came the error, then the trial!"

* *

There are two things men like women to do in a hurry—dress and undress.

* *

A modern boy's the kind who tells his fiancee: "Our marriage won't change a thing. You hold on to your job and I'll keep looking for one."

* *

She: "Here's your ring back! I love another."
He: "What's his name and address?"
She: "Why? Are you going to kill him?"
He: "No, sell him the ring."

* *

My wife and I were making an out-of-town trip to visit an old school friend. He had sent us a letter with detailed instructions on how to get to his house. After driving what seemed like hours, my wife decided to re-read the direction: "Oh, my goodness!" she exclaimed unhappily, "All this time and we've gone only one paragraph."

* *

Then there was a fellow who got badly hurt fighting for his girl's honour. It seemed she wanted to keep it.

* *

"He has a head like a doorknob."
"How come?"
"Any girl can turn it."

35

As the crowded lift descended, the woman became increasingly furious with her husband standing beside her. His face was flushed with delight—because the blonde girl was crowded rather close to him.

As the lift stopped on the ground floor, the blonde suddenly whirled, slapped the man and said: "That'll teach you to pinch!"

Bewildered, the man turned to his wife and protested: "I didn't pinch that girl!"

"Of course, you didn't," said his wife consolingly. "I did!"

* *

One young man to another: "She's the kind of girl you'd like to take home to your stereo."

* *

Want to look young? Mingle with old people.

* *

The postmaster of a certain town received the following letter from a young man of some other town: "I am furnishing below the name and address of a girl who is living in your town whom I am considering marrying although I haven't yet seen her. Please ask the postman who delivers letters in that part of the town to take a good look at her and write to me what he thinks of her."

Dave had just moved into a new flat and decided to get acquainted with the neighbours across the hall. He knocked on the door and was greeted by a young lady, scantily clad and very beautiful.

"Hello," he said, "I'm your new sugar across the hall. Can I borrow a cup of 'neighbour?'"

* *

Overheard: "He thinks she's a bundle of charms— I think she's a bag of tricks!"

* *

They held a beauty competition in the nudist colony. But there was hell to pay when it came to pinning the badges on the winners.

* *

"Do you know what these Red Chinese are up to now? They are making the world's most beautiful girl. They are using Elizabeth Taylor's eyes, Brigitte Bardot's mouth, Marlene Dietrich's legs and Virna Lisi's back."

"Oh boy," moaned a man at the next table, "what couldn't I do with what they are throwing away."

* *

Two of the Women's Lib who were neighbours decided to give up sex in their fight for equal rights. Both their husbands left them and moved into a flat together.

* *

"Now that we are married," he said, "perhaps I can point out a few of your defects."

"Don't bother, dear," she replied. "I know all about them. It's those defects that kept me from getting a better man."

When a young man complains that a young lady has no heart, it is pretty certain that she has his.

* *

Overheard: "She was my secretary before we were married. Now she's the treasurer."

* *

A young accountant stayed late at the office day after day. Finally, the boss called him in and asked for an explanation. "Well, you see sir," he stammered, "my wife works, too—and if I get home before she does, I have to cook the dinner."

* *

Writer Donald Ogden Stewart had a son away at school. When the boy reached the age of 14, he wrote him the following letter: "Dear Son: Now that you have reached the magic age of 14, the time has come to tell you about the bees and flowers. There is a male bee and a female bee, although I haven't the slightest idea which is which. As for the flowers—we got ours from the Plaza Florists, Incorporated. Well, that takes care of that. Write soon. Affectionately, Father."

* *

During our stay in Vienna, we were living next door to a young couple. One evening, the young wife, white as a sheet, called me over to her flat saying that it had been burgled. All the cupboards and drawers were open, with the contents scattered about the floor. The woman wanted to call the police, but I advised her first to inform her husband. And so the case was solved: the young husband had dropped in briefly during business hours to look for his driving licence!

The trouble with being a sexist is that it sounds like more fun than it really is.

* *

"*How well you're looking, Mrs. Smythe*!" "You really think so?" "Indeed I do. There isn't a woman of my acquaintance as old as you who looks nearly as young."

* *

A Sultan kept his harem three miles from where he lived. Every day he sent his man-servant to bring a wife to the palace. The Sultan lived to be 83, but the servant died when he was only 30. The moral of this story is: It's not the women that will kill you, but running after them.

* *

Young bride: "Now, dear, what will I get if I cook a dinner like that for you every day this year?"
Young husband: "My life insurance."

* *

He was explaining Einstein's theory. "It's very simple, this relativity. If a beautiful blonde sits on your lap for an hour, it feels like only a minute. But, if you sit on a hot stove for a minute, it feels like an hour!"

* *

She was only a farmer's daughter—but she tried every salesman's samples.

* *

Rules are the means of a girl's assessing which man she likes well enough to break them for.

First prize at a recent costume ball went to a young woman wearing a maternity jacket over her dress, together with a sign: "I Should Have Danced All Night."

* *

Give some girls an inch and they've got a new bathing suit.

* *

A rather diminutive army officer attended the regimental dance. Arriving late, he saw that everyone was dancing with the exception of one woman. Going up to her and bowing, he said, "May I have the pleasure of this dance?" Looking him up and down she replied rather haughtily, "I don't dance with a child."
Quick as a flash, he retorted: "I am sorry, madam, I was not aware of your condition."

* *

Joe knocked on his girlfriend's door only to hear her cry out, "Can't come, I'm dying."
In panic, Joe burst through the back door to help, and found her dyeing all right—her hair, from brown to blonde.

* *

The boss, seeing his secretary arriving one morning in a very short mini dress:
"Miss Fernandes, don't make it any shorter. I'm a heart patient."

In a jam-packed bus a young secretary was having difficulty fishing for a quarter in her purse to pay her fare. A stalwart gent standing next to her volunteered, "May I pay your fare for you?"

"Oh no," she stammered. "I couldn't let you do that. After all, you're a total stranger."

"Not really," he told her. "You've unzipped me three times."

* *

A boy just starting to date asked a more experienced pal: "What do you do when you have a date with a girl and, after waiting two hours you realize she's stood you up?"

"I send her a note saying, 'I'm sorry I couldn't make it : something came up at the last minute.'"

* *

John: "Whisper those three little words that will make me walk in air."

Rosy: "Go hang yourself!"

* *

He: "Do you think now would be a good time to speak to your father?"

She: "Yes, he's got his shoes off."

* *

Boy: "Am I crazy if I talk to myself?"

Girl: "No, but you are if you listen!"

* *

Rita: "Hello, Willy, I want you to meet my future ex-husband?"

* *

Boy: "Let's play. I'm an explorer and you're the world! Your head is the North Pole and your feet are the South Pole!"

Girl: "Okay, but keep away from the Equator?"

Daughter: "He says he thinks I am the nicest girl in town. Shall I ask him to call?"
Mother: "No, dear, let him keep on thinking so."

* *

Overheard in the chorus girls' dressing room: "Men are all beasts, but I can't help it, I'm an animal lover."

* *

Mother: "But, why the hell did you take your engagement ring back? Wasn't she beautiful?"
Son: "Of course, she was? But she was unreasonable."
Mother: "Unreasonable in what way?"
Son: "She wanted to get married."

* *

"Are they a well-matched couple?" Mrs. Sultan asked her husband.
"Oh, they certainly are," he said. "He snores, and she's deaf."

* *

He—"If you'll give me your telephone number I'll call you up sometime."
She—"It's in the book."
He—"Fine ! What's your name?"
She—"That's in the book, too."

* *

The census taker asked:
"In what state were you when you were born?"
"Well," hesitated the blushing spinster, "er-er-nude."

42

Sweet little thing: "What's the trouble, officer?"
Traffic Cop: "You were going sixty miles an hour Miss, that's all."
Sweet little thing: "Ah, that's where I've got you. I've been out only ten minutes. So, smarty!"

* *

"Why are you so much interested in art studies in the nude?"
"Oh, I guess it is just because I was born that way."

* *

Mack: "Why are you all black and blue this morning?"
Jack: "Last night, I went out with the girl of my dreams and I kept pinching myself to see if I was dreaming!"

* *

The two sexes are male and female. The males are divided into temperate and intemperate, the females into frigid and torrid zones.

* *

Teenage girl to mother: "Dad is at an awkward age. He's too round for his old clothes and too square for the new styles."

* *

Young man to friend: "I'm looking for a beautiful, successful businesswoman whose hobby is housework."

Johnnie was a good dancer and used to visit 'La Paris' almost every night. One night he was introduced to an exceptionally pretty girl. After the introduction was over, the young guy asked her: "Do you dance?"

"I love to," she answered.

"Ah," said the guy. "Then let's love."

* *

One woman to another, as they observe a shapely girl surrounded by men at a party: "She may not be much of a cook, but she sure can stir things up."

* *

A man waiting for the lift in an office building was joined by a smashing-looking young lady. Together, they waited another five minutes for the lift. It was obvious he was trying to think of something to say. Finally, it came to him.

"I think it's beautiful," he said, "our growing old together this way."

* *

And this girl who says: "Every picture tells a story" has never been to the movies in her whole life!"

* *

The average man is more interested in a woman who is interested in him than he is in a woman with beautiful legs.

* *

"Gosh, you have a lovely figure."

"Oh, let's not go over all that again."

The professor was amazed to learn, through various remarks, that Mary, one of his prettiest students, was disliked by the other co-eds.

"Why is Mary so unpopular?" he asked one of the girls."

"Why, she won last year's popularity contest."

* *

Night watchman: "Young man, are you going to kiss that girl.

Student: "No, Sir."

Night watchman: "Well, then, hold my lantern."

* *

Bill: "You dance wonderfully well."

Betty: "I wish I could say the same about you."

Bill: "You could, if you could lie as I do."

* *

"Dammit, daughter," exploded the father, "you can't marry that young man. He doesn't make more than $100 a month."

"Oh, but, Daddy," pleaded the girl, "a month flies by so fast when you're in love with each other."

* *

A dashing young romantic swore by all lover's vows that his Clarice was the fairest maid in all the world, and he would have none other.

"Be mine, Clarice," he pleaded. "If you refuse me, I shall die."

But she refused him, and fifty years later he did die.

Mrs.: "It's a bottle of hair tonic, dear."

Mr.: "Oh, that's very nice of you, darling."

Mrs.: "Yes, I want you to give it to your secretary at the office. Her hair is coming out rather badly on your coat."

* *

There was an angry yelp from the bathroom.

"What's the matter, dear?" asked the little bride.

"It's my razor blade," he yelled. "It's dull. It won't cut at all."

"Why, that's silly," she said. "Your whiskers can't possibly be tougher than my lead pencil."

* *

Mrs. Newlywed: "Oh George, do order a rat trap to be sent home today."

Mr. Newlywed: "But you bought one last week."

Mrs. Newlywed: "Yes, dear, but there's a rat in that."

* *

Girl: "But, darling, be reasonable! After all, we can't live on love."

Boy: "I don't see why not. Your family loves you."

* *

He: "Say something soft and sweet to me."

She: "Custard pie."

* *

Sometimes a girl can attract a man with her mind, but it's easier to attract him with what she doesn't mind.

* *

When a girl loses her head, it usually ends up on someone's pillow.

Girl: "Just think, darling, the preacher only mumbles a few words and we're married."
Guy: "It is true, and just think, a few words mumbled in my sleep and we are divorced."

* *

She: "Am I really the only girl you've ever kissed?"
He: "Certainly—and by far the prettiest."

* *

Angry father: "What do you mean by bringing my daughter home at 3 o' clock in the morning?"
Mild suitor: "Well, sir, I have to be at work at 7."

* *

Optimistic bachelor: "Let's get married."
Pessimistic spinster: "Good Lord! Who'd have us?"

* *

Bride: "Do you still take an interest in everything I do?"
Groom: "Certainly, darling. For example, I've spent all day wondering what you put in those biscuits we had at breakfast."

* *

"Say, that chorus girl you introduced me to seemed a pretty hard type."
"Hard? Why, a diamond is the only thing that makes an impression on her."

* *

Again there was this school girl who was cross-eyed so that when she cried, the tears from her left eye fell on her right cheek.

47

A student in a college hostel ran out of funds.
He telegraphed his dad:
NO FUN NO MUN YOUR SON.
Promptly came the reply: SO BAD SO SAD YOUR
DAD.

* *

Washington State collegian bragging: "Why man,
we've got a telescope in our observatory so strong
you can see a pretty girl 2000 miles away!"

* *

The College professor was talking about girls. He
said: "Some girls are like cigarettes; they come in
packs, get lit, make you puff, go out unexpectedly,
leave a bad taste in your mouth, and still they
satisfy."

* *

A farmer advised his daughter: "When it comes to
going out with drugstore cowboys know what to do,
know how to do, know when to do, but don't do
it."

* *

Then there was the model who sat on a broken
bottle and cut a good figure.

* *

An attractive woman hurried into a psychiatrist's
office. "I'm in love with a wonderful man and he
is in love with me," she said. "Both our parents
are agreeable to the marriage and we feel certain
that we will be happy."

"Well," said the psychiatrist, "what's your problem?"

"Oh doctor," she moaned. "I just don't know what
to tell my husband."

Man (showing snapshot of himself with a fish to neighbour): "But my daughter really caught a big fish on our vacation—a young man 22 years old."

* *

The beautiful young lady went to the psychiatrist's office for her first visit. The doctor looked at her for a few seconds. Then e said, "Come over here please."
He promptly put his arm around her and kissed her. As he finally released her, she commented briskly, "That takes care of my problem. Now what's yours?"

* *

A young married woman wanted her new maid to be pleased with her position. "You'll have an easy time of it here," she said, "since we have no children to annoy you."
"Oh, I like children," said the maid. "Don't go restricting yourself on my account."

* *

She: "Is horse racing a clean sport?"
He: "Well, it cleans quite a few every day."

* *

The ambitious young bachelor entered the marriage broker's establishment. "May I see a photo of the lady with $50,000?" he asked.
"Sorry," said the broker. "No pictures of ladies with over $10,000."

She reminded me of brown sugar—she was so sweet and refined.

* *

"Don't I look good in tails?"
"Why not? Your ancestors did."

* *

A tall, well-built girl was applying for a job. In the course of inquiring into her work history, she was asked if she had any physical handicaps.
"No," she replied, drawing herself up proudly, "they're all assets."

* *

"I don't know how you carry on with three girls in your office!"
"Simple, I give leave to two at the same time."

* *

A pretty young girl who joined the military was asked by the Captain, how she liked military life.
"It's like this," she summed it up. "Yes-sir," all day and "No-sir," all night.

* *

"A beautiful young girl who is a good football player wants to give me a date. Should I go with her?"
"Only be careful about her kicks!"

* *

KISS is an invited disease.

Carve/Curve
i.e. Character and Constitution

Two negroes bought a watch between them. It did not show the correct time, so one of them took it to pieces and found a dead fly inside. "No wonder the watch would not go," he said. "The engine driver is dead."

* *

The story is told of one irate tax-payer who, while filing his income-tax returns, frankly wrote: "Very mean" against the query: "Nature of tax-payer."

A Scot died and left his uncle all the money the latter owed him!

* *

The politicians of opposing parties are discussing their strategy. The Democrat says: "I'm forever promoting. For example, whenever I take a cab, I give the cabbie a large tip and say: 'Vote for Democratic.'"

The Republican says: " My approach is similar. Whenever I take a cab, I don't give the driver any tip at all and I leave him wit h: "Don't forget to vote Democratic."

* *

A young man foolishly twitted a much older man on his age. The older man looked at him and said: "Young man, an ass is older at twenty than a man at sixty."

* *

A joke on Capitol Hill: In Socialism you have two cows—one is given to your neighbour. In Communism you have two cows—the Government takes both and shoots you. In Democracy, the Government buys both cows, shoots one, milks the other, throws the milk away and buys butter from Holland.

* *

President: "Why did you engage that man as cashier? He squints, has a crooked nose and outstanding ears."

Manager: "Well, he'll be so easy to identify if he absconds."

Plagiarism: Only form of stealing in which the thief leaves his name.

* *

Relatives: People who never leave you alone with your happiness.

* *

Virgin: A girl who hasn't met her maker.

* *

Do you know the difference between the English, the Scottish and the Irish?"
"No, what's it?"
"Well, on leaving a train, an Irishman walks of without looking to see whether he's left anything behind; an Englishman looks back to see whether he's left anything; and a Scotsman looks back to see whether anybody else has left anything."

* *

Hypochondriac: One who can't leave being well enough alone.

* *

Tightrope-walker: Man who keeps to the straight-and-narrow.

* *

Son-in-law: Man who until his marriage did not suspect how many shortcomings he suffered from.

* *

"My uncle is a butcher. He's six feet tall and wears size-twelve shoes. What does he weigh?"
"Meat, of course."

53

An Englishman, an Irishman and a Scotsman met in a bar and, after several rounds of whisky, became well inebriated. Suddenly, the impulsive Englishman fished out a £10 note from his pocket and, striking a match, burnt it completely. "Let's see you guys better that!" he bragged.

Not to be outdone, the Irishman took out a £100 note and, in a similar manner, reduced it to ashes.

Came the Scotsman's turn and he coolly extracted his cheque-book. He wrote out a cheque for £1,000, signed it—and then burnt it in full view of his companions!

* *

Little Bobby was called from his play to meet a visitor.

"How old are you, little man?" he was asked.

"I'm at the awkward age," he replied.

"Really?" asked the visitor. "What do you mean by awkward age?"

"Too old to cry and too young to swear."

* *

George Bernard Shaw is reputed to have granted an interview to a young journalist who, while reading aloud his book to him, looked up on Shaw's opening the window. "Do you want the neighbours to hear my book as well?" brightly enquired the journalist.

"No, but, since my youth, I have been in the habit of sleeping with open windows."

* *

A man asked a boy how old he was.

"Twelve," was the reply.

"Hmm," remarked the man, "you are well-built for your age."

"I ought to be," retorted the boy. "My father is an architect."

54

America's Brigadier-General, Samuel Griffith, comments on China: "The only predictable thing about Chinese events is that unpredictable events will occur with predictable regularity."

* *

Youth: A delicacy you gulp down without stopping to savour.

* *

"If I were the sort of man," said Sir Henry Wood, "who never answered letters, forgot appointments and didn't know where to lay his hands on things, they would call me an artist. Because I'm not, they call me a disciplinarian."

* *

A sorter in a post office abstained from work. When asked for an explanation, he replied: "I was feeling out of sorts!"

* *

Adult: A person who has stopped growing at both ends and started growing in the middle.

* *

Connoisseur: A man who collects old masters and young mistresses.

* *

Soft soap is the best thing for dirty looks.

* *

Advantages of baldness: (1) When somebody arrives unexpectedly, all you have to do is straighten your tie. (2) No one can tell you hair-raising stories.

It was once remarked to Lord Chesterfield that man is the only creature endowed with the power of laughter. "True," said the peer, "and you may add, perhaps, that he is the only creature that deserve   be laughed at."

* *

An American and a Scotsman were discussing the cold experienced in winter in the North of Scotland. "Why, it's nothing at all compared to the cold we have in the United States," said the American. "I can recollect one winter when a sheep, jumping from a hillock into a field, became suddenly frozen on the way and stuck in the air like a mass of ice." "But man," exclaimed the Scotsman, "the law of gravity wouldn't allow that."

"I know," replied the American, "but the law of gravity was frozen too!"

* *

Which animal travels with the most and which with the least luggage? The elephant the most, because he never travels without a trunk. The fox and the rooster the least, because they have one brush and comb between them.

* *

"One day at a cabinet meeting," recalls former Israeli Prime Minister Golda Meir, "we were discussing the increase of night-time attacks on women. One minister proposed   curfew—women were to stay home after dark. But,   said, it's the men who are attacking the women! If we   c a curfew, it will have to   nen who stay home, not the women."

A passenger on the Frontier Mail, on being asked if he was comfortable, etc., stated that the train was running punctually, his berth was comfortable, but he had been seated at lunch adjacent to a cross-eyed fellow passenger who continually ate from the wrong plate.

* *

An American, while placing a bunch of flowers on a grave, saw an old Chinese placing a bowl of rice on an adjacent grave. With a superior smile the American asked: "When do you think your friend will come up to eat his dinner?"

With a beatific smile, the old Chinese replied: "The same time as your friend comes up to smell the flowers!"

* *

Once upon a time, Sandy Jameson was walking along a busy highway when he came upon the scene of an automobile accident. Several injured men were still lying about on the road.

The Scotsman approached one of the victims and asked: "Has the insurance man been around here?"

"No."

"Well then," said the Scot. "I'll just lie down here by your side."

* *

Two little Hollywood boys were exchanging taunts.

"My father can beat your father," said one.

"My father is your father!" replied the other.

Lou: "Now, is your brother really near-sighted?"
Stu: "I'll say he is—he counts elephants in his sleep!"

* *

Near the water cooler: "The only thing I ever learnt from experience is that I'd just made another mistake."

* *

Man to neighbour: "My father believed in stern discipline. If I did something wrong, he provided the discipline and I provided the stern."

* *

Happiness is the shortest distance between two disappointments.

* *

In our military academy, we had a civilian chemistry teacher who was very particular about cadets saluting him. One day he reprimanded a cadet who had failed to salute him.
That same evening he complained to a colleague: "I really can't understand it. When I'm alone no one salutes me; when I'm with my wife, half the academy salutes me; and when I'm with my daughter, every cadet salutes me!"

* *

Since she's a photographer's daughter, she sits in a dark room and just awaits developments.

An American soldier riding on a bus in Sweden told the man sitting next to him: "America is the most democratic country in the world. Ordinary citizens may go to the White House to see the President and discuss things with him."

The man said, "That's nothing. In Sweden, the king and the people ride in the same bus."

When the man got off the bus, the American was told by other passengers that he had been sitting next to King Gustaf VI Adolf!

* *

"You know," says the East German to the West German, "the essential difference between you and us consists in your treasuring the money while we treasure the people."

"Correct," replies the West German. "So we lock up our money and you lock up your people."

* *

Temperamental: Ninety percent temper, ten percent mental.

* *

"What happened to you? Your face is all cut up."
"I went to a barbers' college to be shaved and one of the students failed in his examination on me."

* *

The little girl on TV announced : "The one I want to be when I grow up is Marilyn Monroe because she's famous all over."

Sherlock Holmes went to heaven. Saint Peter asked:
"What's your claim?"

"I claim to be the world's greatest detective," said
Holme

"Pass a test and you can stay in heaven," said St.
Peter.

"What test?"

"There are millions of people here. If you can pick
out Adam and Eve you win."

Holmes had no difficulty: they were the only ones
without navels.

* *

A famous man unveiled a statue of himself: Asked
later how he felt about it, he said, "I find myself
ha   geons."

* *

A politician said to Horace Greeley one day:
"I am a self-made man."

"That, sir," replied Greeley, "relieved the Almighty
o   terrible responsibility."

* *

A Scot went into a shop and bought a briefcase.
"Shal I wrap it up for you?" asked the clerk.

"No, thank you," he said. "Just put the paper and
strin inside."

*

A French husband is very sensitive to the feelings of
affection. "He first kisses the fingertips, then the
shoulder, and then the back of the neck...."

'By tha   said an American girl, "an
American husband returns from his honeymoon."

"You should be ashamed of yourself for laughing at that fat man."
"I'm just having fun at his expanse."

* *

She: "How many times a day do you shave?"
He: "Oh, forty or fifty times."
She: "Say, are you crazy?"
He: "No, I'm a barber."

* *

Her mouth was so big, everytime she yawned her ears disappeared!

* *

An optimist is a man who goes to the window in the morning and says, "Good morning, God." A pessimist goes to the window and says, "My God, it's morning."

* *

The Bombay big shot was in an explosive mood. "I want a super 'colossal picture,' one that'll burst in the audience's faces like a bomb!"

* *

Two men, members of a religious order, wanted to smoke while walking in the garden.
They agreed that each would ask his superior for permission. The first one returned to find the second one smoking and complained indignantly, "I was refused."
"What did you ask?" inquired the second one.
"I asked if I could smoke while meditating."
"Oh," said the other, blowing his smoke reflectively, "I asked if I could meditate while smoking."

61

An ambitious mother wrote to director Alfred Hitchcock, "I have a perfectly beautiful daughter. She is 17 years old, 5 ft. 5 in. tall, and weighs 120 lbs. Do you think she might succeed in the movies?" To which Hitchcock replied, "Madam, it would be impossible to say, as you did not state her width."

* *

An Englishman and an American were out for a walk.
After half an hour's silence, the Englishman remarked "Spring in the air!"
"Why should I?" asked the American.

* *

"Why do artists all put their signature at the bottom of their paintings?" asked a little boy.
"That way everybody knows which side is up," replied his father.

* *

"Grandma do your eyeglasses magnify things?" a little girl asked.
"Why, yes, they do," said her grandmother.
"Then would you take them off before you cut a piece of cake for me?" asked the little girl.

* *

Abraham Lincoln once said: "If you can't find something in the ordinary dictionary or the encyclopaedia, you might try the provision vote."

General Patton, who like Napoleon believed the best defence was a good offence, is said to have illustrated with this story the fate of timidity in a commander: "Lincoln, growing impatient to the point of exasperation with McClellan's 'waiting campaign' wrote to his hesitant general:

'My dear McClellan: If you don't want to use the army, I should like to borrow it for a while.'

"Yours respectfully,
A. Lincoln."

* *

When Thomas Jefferson presented his credentials as U.S. Minister to France, the French Premier remarked, "I see that you have come to replace Benjamin Franklin." "I have come to succeed him," corrected Jefferson. "No one can replace him."

* *

Clever person: One who puts his problems away for a brainy day.

* *

Parents: People who lie awake wondering if daughter's dream boat is one of those ships that pass in the night.

* *

Intoxication: To feel sophisticated and not be able to pronounce it.

* *

A mother brought her four-year-old twins to a store for a final fitting of identical coats. "Wouldn't the twins like to see themselves in the mirror?" the store owner asked.

"Oh, that won't be necessary," the mother replied. "They never do—they look at each other."

Once, an Englishman, an Arab and an American were standing on a street corner in Cairo when a spectacular Oriental beauty sided by.

"By Jove!" exclaimed the Englishman.

The Arabi murmured a fervent, "By Allah!"

And the American said, softly, "By tomorrow night."

* *

Charles de Gaulle once said: "When I am right, I get angry. Churchill gets angry when he is wrong. So we were very often angry at each other."

* *

Druggist: "Can I offer you something for that cold of yours, Mr. Ryan?"

Ryan: "Faith, and if ye want it, it is for nothing ye can be having it."

* *

"Abstinence," said Father Magee, "is a wonderful thing, Dennis."

"Sure and it is, Father," said Dennis, "if practised in moderation."

* *

Proud father: "Yes, sir, our household represents the whole United Kingdom. I am English, my wife's Irish, the nurse represents Scotland, and the baby wails."

* *

Woman is attractive at 20, attentive at 30, and adhesive at 40.

Q. Why is sex so popular?
A. Because it is centrally situated.

* *

MONSOON is a French gentleman.

* *

WAVES are sailors who go down to the sea in ships.

* *

HUMAN BEINGS are modern animals.

* *

AUSTRALIAN is a typical old-fashioned Southern Gentleman who hadn't embraced his wife for six months, but shot another man who did.

* *

DIPLOMAT is a man who says Yes when he means Perhaps and says Perhaps when he means No. And the man who says No is no diplomat.

* *

HERO is a battle-scarred man.

* *

From discussing the physical peculiarities of Douglas, who was a very small man, a group of Lincoln's friends turned to the question of how long a man's legs should be. Upon Lincoln's joining the group, he was asked the question.

"Well," he said, "I should think a man's legs ought to be long enough to reach from his body to the ground."

Someone asked Lincoln once whether he did not find the ceremonies of the Presidency irksome.
"Yes, sometimes," said Lincoln. "In fact, I feel sometimes like a man who was ridden out of town on a rail, and said: 'If it wasn't for the honour of the thing, I'd rather walk!'"

* *

ELECTRICIAN: A man who wires you for money.

* *

BOSS: The man who is early when you are late, and late when you are early.

* *

OPTIMIST: A person who lights a match before asking you for a cigarette.

* *

Voltaire stopped, faced the crowd and cried: "Englishmen! Am I not punished enough in not being an Englishman?"
The crowd cheered wildly and then proceeded to provide him safe conduct back to his dwelling.

* *

It was an exhibition of pictures in modern art. He waited in front of a painting admiringly and said to the artist: "How realistic! It makes my mouth water."
Artist: "A sunset makes your mouth water?"
Visitor: "Dear me, I thought it was a fried egg!"

* *

An optimist : A man who gets married when he's seventy-five and then looks for a house near a school.

A diplomat is a man who can convince his wife she looks vulgar in diamonds.

* *

Parents are the people who bear infants, bore teen-agers and board newlyweds.

* *

A gypsy and a hippie had an argument as to who could withstand foul smell longer. They decided to remain with a skunk in a small pen. First the gypsy went in. He ran out in desperation after a couple of minutes. Then the hippie took his turn. After a minute, the skunk bolted !

* *

The meanest Scotsman in the world was the one who fired a revolver on Christmas eve outside the door, then came in and told his children that Father Christmas had committed suicide !

* *

A Scot was engaged in an argument with a conductor as to whether the fare was five or ten cents. Finally the disgruntled conductor picked up the Scotsman's suitcase and tossed it off the train, just as it passed over a bridge. It landed with a splash. "Man," screamed the Scot, "isn't it enough to try to overcharge me, but now you try to drown my little boy !"

* *

Sham : "My brother sometimes changes clothes even four or five times in one hour ?"
Ram : "How old is he?"
Sham : "Eight months."

Mistress : "And above all I want obedience and truthfulness."

New maid: "Yes, madam. But if anybody calls when you are in, and you want me to say that you are out, which comes first—obedience or truthfulness?"

Edit / Educe
i.e. Education and Endeavour

Lady Teacher: "What tense is 'I am beautiful?'"
Junior: "Past."

* *

Joe: "Did you hear about the man who suddenly
went blind while drinking his coffee?"
Moe: "No, I didn't. What happened?"
Joe: "He left his spoon in his cup."

"Did you hear about the fellow who invented a device for looking through walls?"
"No. I didn't. What does he call it?"
"A window."

* *

Visitor: "And how old are you, my little man?"
Little man: "Well, it's like this. The latest aptitude test shows my psychological age to be 12; my moral age to be 4; anatomical age to be 7 and my physiological age to be 6. I suppose, however, you want to know my chronological age: that's 8."

* *

"Where did the car hit him?" asked the coroner.
"At the junction of the dorsal and cervical vertebrae," replied the medical witness.
The burly foreman rose from his seat. "I've lived in these parts for fifty years," he protested ponderously "and I have never heard of the place."

* *

An incorrigible youngster was hauled before the principal for having told his teacher to go to that four-letter place where they have no snow.
The principal explained to him that such language could not be tolerated, but that if he would apologise to his teacher, she might give him another chance.
The boy was too stubborn to back down completely. Finally, however, between sniffles, he managed to make some concession: "Miss Peters," he said, "you don't need to go there now."

Teacher: "So you are the boy who wrote on the board: 'Teacher is a fool?' "

Pupil: "Yes, sir."

Teacher: "Well, at least I am glad you have told the truth."

* *

"I am working for the support of literature."

"Oh, what are you doing?"

"Making bookcases."

* *

A ten-year-old boy was asked by his teacher to spell straight. He spelt it correctly. Then his teacher asked: "What does it mean?"

The kid replied: "Without soda and water."

* *

The teacher had written a number with a decimal point on the blackboard and, to show the effect of multiplying by ten, had rubbed out the decimal point. "Now, Alfred," she said, "where is the decimal point?"

"On the duster!" was the reply.

* *

"I am worried about you being at the bottom of your class," said the father.

"Don't worry about it, Dad," assured his son. "They teach the same thing at both ends."

* *

He: "Excuse me, stewardess. How high is this plane?"

She: "About thirty thousand feet."

He: "Oh! And how wide is it?"

"When was the radio first mentioned in the Bible?"
"When the Lord took a rib from Adam and made a loudspeaker!"

* *

Asked to submit a short note on 'pocket money,' a schoolboy wrote: "It's the only thing that never stays in my pocket."

* *

Author: "Here is the manuscript I offered you last year."
Editor: "What's the idea of bringing this thing back when I rejected it last year?"
Author: "Well, you see, you've had a year's experience since then."

* *

"So you got your poem printed?"
"Yes", replied the author. "I sent the first stanza to the editor of the Correspondence Column with the inquiry, 'Can anyone give me the rest of this poem?'" Then I sent in the complete poem under another name."

* *

Adam and Eve must have been the first communists because they had nothing to wear, nothing to eat but an apple and lived in paradise.

* *

"Good gracious!" shouted the teacher. "I ask you a simple question: "What's a fortification?" He got no answer—all the boys sat glum. The teacher was exasperated. Pointing to a boy, he said: "Now what's a fortification?"
The boy got up and answered: "Twice twentification, Sir."

The teacher was trying to popularise arithmetic by bringing home the examples to the pupils.

Teacher: "Now, if you had fiver upees in one pocket and ten rupees in the other, what would you say you had?"

Pupil: "The wrong pants."

**

Reader: Person whose TV is at the repairers.

**

The teacher had explained the grammatical term, the error of proximity. Then he asked Sam to give an example.

Sam: "When the boss takes his steno-secretary on his knee, that's an error of proximity."

**

Teacher: "If there are five flies on a table and you kill one, how many would remain?"

Mario: "One—the dead one."

**

So far nobody has invented an intelligence test to equal matrimony.

**

The teacher had been giving a talk on the importance of milk. When she finished, she asked Shekhar to name six things with milk in them.

"Three cows!" was the startling answer

**

The little boy got separated from his father in a crowd and told a policeman he was lost. The policeman asked:

"What's your father like?"

"Wine and women."

The class was studying nutrition. When Asad handed in his homework, the teacher said: "Asad, you were supposed to write a five-page essay on milk but you only did one page."

"I know," Asad answered. "I was writing about condensed milk."

* *

Teacher: "Give an example of a hypocrite."
Pupil: "A boy who goes to school with a smile on his face."

* *

A father was telling his neighbour how he stopped his son from being late to high school. "I bought him a car," the father said.

"How did that stop him from being late?" the neighbour asked.

"Why, he's got to get there early to find a parking place."

* *

"Mummy, am I descended from a monkey."
"I don't know. I've never met your father's people."

* *

In public schools today, the teacher is afraid of the principal; the principals are afraid of the superintendents; the superintendents are afraid of the school board; the board is afraid of the parents; the parents are afraid of the children; and the children are afraid of nobody!

* *

Teacher: "What's etiquette, John?"
John: "Etiquette is the noise you don't make when you are eating your soup."

Teacher: "Can anyone tell me why Adam bit the apple in the garden of Eden?"
Pupil: "Because he had no knife, Teacher."

* *

A budding poet to the editor of a paper: "Please read the enclosed poem very carefully and return it to me with your comments as soon as possible as I have other irons in the fire."
Came the reply: "Remove irons; insert poems."

* *

An English master, confronted with what to put in a boy's report when he knew the child was cheating but couldn't prove it finally wrote: "Forging steadily ahead."

* *

Son: "Daddy, why did you put your thumb impression on my progress report instead of your signature?"
Father: "I don't want your teacher to think that anyone with your marks could possibly have a father who can read or write."

* *

"I read your long article on insomnia, Dr. Harry."
"Interesting?"
"It sent me to sleep."

* *

Plagiarism: Only form of stealing in which the thief leaves his name.

The book editor of a publishing firm turned down a young mystery writer's manuscript. "It's no good," he argued. "There isn't a single corpse in your book. You ought to know that it's death that gives life to a novel."

* *

Jones: "That Editor returned my verses."
Smith: "What for?"
Jones: "For no rhyme or reason, I'm sure."

* *

A small boy returned home from school and told his father he was now second in his class. The top place was held by a girl. "But surely Ram," said the mother. "you're not going to be beaten by a mere girl?"
"Well, you see, Mother," explained Ram, "girls are not nearly so 'mere' as they used to be."

* *

I was taking my nine-year-old daughter to a Girl Scouts Camp for her first experience away from home. En route, I told her that she should make every effort to be kind to the other girls in her tent. "Honey, if you see somone sitting in the corner, alone and nervous, be sure to be friendly and make her feel at home."
"I will, Mother," she replied thoughtfully. Then she added, "But what if that someone sitting in that corner is me?"

Teacher: "What's this painting of yours supposed to show?"

Pupil: "It's a cow eating grass in a meadow."

Teacher: "But where's the grass?"

Pupil: "Why, the cow's eaten it all."

Teacher. "Where then is the cow?"

Pupil: "It's just gone to another meadow to look for more grass."

* *

A young teacher appeared for his first job interview at a village school. The members of the school board quizzed him thoroughly on the acceptability of his views. At last, one of the elders asked: "We heard a lot of talk that the world is round, while others reckon it appears to be flat. How do you feel about it?"

The young man anxious for the job, quickly replied: "I can teach it either way!"

* *

On college campus: "He took just one karate lesson, and he already can break boards—with his cast."

* *

Little Jimmy was found by his father in the barn shaking his pet rabbit and saying: "Five and five. How much is five and five?"

The surprised father interrupted the proceedings and asked: "What's the meaning of all this, Jimmy?"

"Oh," said Jimmy. "Teacher told us that rabbits multiply rapidly, but this one can't even add."

* *

The trouble with being a teacher is that you have to be perfect so early in the morning.

"With a single stroke of the brush," said the school teacher, taking his class through the art gallery, "Sir Joshua Reynolds could change a smiling face into a frowning one."

"So can my mother," said a small boy.

* *

Teacher: "How do you like your new house?"

Student: "Oh, we like it very much. I have a room of my own, each of my sisters has a room of her own. But poor Mum, she's still in with Dad."

* *

From which book have you benefited the most?" a reporter asked George Bernard Shaw.

"My cheque book," replied Shaw.

* *

Jane: "How old are you?"

Mabel: "I just turned twenty-three."

Jane: "I get it. Thirty-two."

* *

My young nephew returned from school one day and said that he had fallen down during recess and grazed his knees and elbow. "Didn't you cry?" I asked him. "No" he replied bravely. "The bell rang and there was no time."

* *

"Do you think I should put more fire into my editorials?" the writer asked.

"No," said his editor. "Vice versa."

* *

Editor: "Did you write this poem yourself?"

Contributor: "Yes, every line of it."

Editor: "Then I'm glad to meet you, Edgar Allan Poe, I thought you were dead long ago."

Author: "Well, sir, the upshot of it was that it took me ten years to discover that I had absolutely no talent for writing literature."

Friend: "You gave up?"

Author: "Oh, no, by that time I was too famous."

"You've read my last book, haven't you?" asked the author.

"I hope so," groaned the critic.

* *

First composer: "Where did you get the main theme for your Second Symphony?"

Second composer: "From the swing arrangement of my First."

* *

G.K. Chesterton and several other literary figures were asked one evening what book they would prefer to have with them if stranded on a desert isle.

"The complete works of Shakespeare," said one writer without hesitation.

"I'd choose the Bible," interrupted another. "How about you?" someone asked Chesterton.

"I would choose," replied the author, "Thomas's Guide to Practical Shipbuilding!"

* *

Author: "I'm convinced that the publishers have a conspiracy against me."

Friend: "What makes you think so?"

Author: "Ten of them have refused the same story."

A schoolboy's left arm was badly injured and he went to a doctor and asked him to bandage his right arm.

Doctor: "Bandage the right arm! Why?"

Schoolboy: "You don't know school children. They will attack the bandaged arm."

* *

A small Indian boy appeared in the class of a Lambeth, London, school teacher for the first time and she asked him his name. "Venkataratanam Narasimha Rattaiah." he said. When she asked. "How do you spell it?" he replied, "My mother helps me."

* *

On the difference between reading a book on physical medicine and one on psychiatry: in the first case, the reader thinks he has all the symptoms; in the second, he thinks his friends are typical examples.

* *

Grandpa: "Who's the most popular boy in your school?"

Jack: "Last term young Jones was. He gave us all the measles."

* *

Bobby: "Dad what are those holes in the board for?"

Dad: "Those are knot holes."

Bobby: "Well, if they are not holes, what are they?"

* *

"What was the hardest thing you learned at college?" asked the proud father.

"How to open beer bottles with a quarter," said the son.

Tessie: "What is your brother in college?"
Jessie: "A half-back."
Tessie: "I mean in his studies."
Jessie: "Oh, in his studies he's away back."

** **

Tryout: "What's the Board of Student 'Publications?"
Editor: "Any group of people who can see three meanings in a college joke that has only two meanings.

Feel Fix
i.e. Friend and Foe

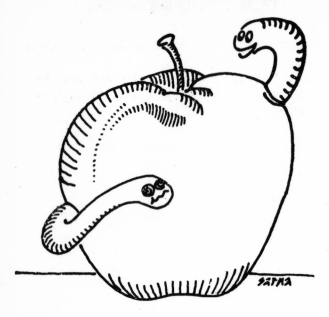

A worm was coming out of a hole in an apple and he saw another worm looking at him. "I love you," he said.

"Don't be silly. I'm your other end."

** **

Two friends, who had not seen each other for a long time, were telling each other about their homes.

Said one: "When I have an argument with my wife, I always have the last word."

Second: "I am glad to hear it. Will you tell me how you manage it?"

First: "It's easy. I simply apologise!"

"Halt?" said the bandit, pointing a revolver at the learned professor. "If you move, you're dead?"

"My man," said the professor, unperturbed, "you should be more exact in your statement. If I move, it would be a positive sign that I was alive!"

* *

Two friends, who hadn't seen each other in several years, met on the street. "Who are you working for now?" asked the first.

"Same people," answered the other. "My wife and four children."

* *

Man to friend: "You might describe my financial situation as fluid. Which is a sort of nice way of saying I'm going down the drain."

* *

Man to friend: "By the time I found out my father was right, my son was old enough to disagree with me."

*

After a busy day at a department store, one weary salesgirl remarked to her friend, "The more patience I have, the more people use it."

* *

A man complained to a friend: "My wife Ida likes to talk things over—and over, and over, and over."

* *

"Remember," the minister warned his friend who was about to sign a television contract, "the big print giveth and the small print taketh away."

* *

An understanding friend defines a well-balanced girl as one with an empty head and a full sweater.

Neighbours: People who know more about **you** than you do yourself.

* *

Two neighbours met. "I see your wife has a **new** mink coat. That ought to keep her warm."
"I didn't buy that to keep her warm," said **the** other, "just to keep her quiet."

* *

"He says he is closely related to you?"
"He's a fool?"
"Then he must be."

* *

A friend asked a lady: "I suppose you carry a memento of some sort in that locket of yours?"
"Yes, a strand of my husband's hair."
"But your husband's still alive."
"Yes, but his hair's gone."

* *

Frank: "When I woke up this morning, I felt like going out and getting a job."
Hank: "Did you?"
Frank: "No. I stayed in bed until the feeling passed."

* *

Freshman: "How about a battle of wits?"
Senior : "Sorry, I never attack an unarmed man. '

* *

A father returning from a camping trip with five children says it's great to be home and away from the overcrowding of the wide open spaces.

According to the UPI : "Police battled a gang of bandits in Southern Thailand. One bandit was killed. A police spokesman said the battle began when the bandit gang disguised as policemen, challenged a group of policemen disguised as bandits."

* *

My friend has read so much about the terrible effects of smoking that he's decided to give up reading altogether.

* *

An outdoor man who had gone on hunting expeditions all over the world—always accompanied by his wife on her insistence—told his trouble to a friend one day. "Yes sir," said the hunter, "I've taken that woman into the jungles of Africa, the jungles of Borneo and the jungles of Malaya. The only trouble is she always finds her way back."

* *

A little ant was racing round and round a medium-sized cracker-box. His pal, another ant, observing the first ant, couldn't understand what the furious hurry was about, so he asked his running friend: "Just what's your hurry, pal?"
The first ant replied: "Well, there's a sign here that says: TEAR ALONG THE DOTTED LINE."

* *

It's a common pratice to criticize noisy neighbours, but they are the best crime protection your house can have.

When the ticket examiner came to our compartment, my friend discovered that he had left his season ticket behind at home.

Trying to joke his way out of the situation, he told the examiner, "I'm not a dishonest fellow—look, my face is my ticket."

"My duty, friend," replied the unrelenting TE, "is to punch every ticket."

* *

A college friend of mine was well known for making the unexpected visit, after which, if the person he wanted to see wasn't in, he would pin a note on the door.

The tables were turned when one day he was rushed to hospital for an emergency operation. Four of us went to his bedside, but he was still unconscious from the anaesthetic. After waiting for a while, we pinned a note to his sheets: "Dear Gareth. We called but you were out."

* *

Two partners of a big Melbourne business were on a fishing trip when a sudden storm capsized the boat. One could swim, the other floundered helplessly.

"Bill," cried the swimmer.

"Can you float alone?"

"Look Jim," gulped the non-swimmer, "this is no time to be talking business."

* *

Then there was a germ whose friends avoided him because he'd caught a dose of penicillin.

"How did you make your neighbour keep his hens in his own yard?"

"One night I hid half a dozen eggs under a bush in my garden, and the next day I let him see me gather them."

* *

Between the golden years of youth and the golden years of retirement come those nickel-plated years when you do all the work.

* *

First nut: "Did you hear that joke about the Egyptian guide who showed some tourists two skulls of Cleopatra—one as a child and one as a woman?"

Second nut: "No, let's hear it."

* *

When a young French girl came to stay with us recently, our neighbour invited her out to tea. Having eaten to her heart's content, she was offered another slice of cake.

"No, thank you," she replied, "I am fed up."

* *

Three deaf ladies were travelling on top of an open bus.

"Windy, isn't it?" said one.

"No, it isn't Wednesday, it's Thursday," said the second.

"Yes, I'm thirsty too. Let's all get off and have something to drink," said the third.

Jones: "Good evening, old man. Thought I'd drop in and see you about the umbrella you borrowed from me last week."
Brown: "I'm sorry, but I lent it to a friend of mine. Were you wanting it?"
Jones: "Well, not for myself, but the fellow I borrowed it from says the owner wants it."

* *

Old boy: "I feel like a two-year-old this morning.
Young man: "Horse, child or egg?"

* *

Hokum: "No getting around it. There's one fellow you have to take your hat off to."
Yokum: "Who is that?"
Hokum: "The barber."

* *

A gentleman feeling a bit fed up with life decided to commit suicide by hanging himself. A friend came into the room and discovered him standing with a rope around his waist, and he inquired what he was trying to do. The gentleman told him he was taking his own life. "But the rope around your waist....?" said his friend, puzzled.
"It hurts around the neck," complained the gentle man.

* *

Wife: "Mrs. Rasp invited us to her muscial, and I think we ought to do something to reciprocate."
Husband: "You mean retaliate, don't you?"

Nixon: "This fellow Smythe claims to be a relative of yours, and says he can prove it."
Dixon: "That man's a fool."
Nixon: "That may be a mere coincidence."

* *

Wife: "One more of these drinks and I'll be feeling it."
Husband: "One more of these drinks and I'll be letting you!"

* *

On his return from a trip abroad, a friend told me: "The hotel was so cold, you just held the toothbrush and your teeth did the rest."

* *

I chided my friend for making such a fuss over her little French poodle. "I can't help it," she explained. "After all he is an only dog."

* *

Middle-aged matron to neighbour: "I'm afraid I don't do as much gardening as I used to. These days the ground seems to be much lower down."

* *

The scene in the film was tense and the audience sat enthralled. Suddenly the hero slapped the heroine on the fall.
In the silence that followed, a young voice piped up: "Why doesn't she hit back like you do, mummy?"

* *

A snorer in a Russian movie-house was disturbing the audience.
When patrons yelled to cut it out, the snorer snapped, "I paid for the seat and I'll do as I please!"

Let us be thankful for the fools, but for them, the rest of us could not succeed.

* *

Friend: "Ah, professor, I hear your wife has had twins. Boys or girls?"
Prof (absent-mindedly): "Well, I believe one is a girl, and one a boy, but it may be the other way round."

* *

"What makes you look so pale and sad?" an older friend asked the romantic boy.
"It's terrible," confessed the youth. "She's the most wonderful girl in the world. And finally I—I got up enough courage to ask her to marry me, and she refused."
"Cheer up!" said the friend. "A woman's 'no' may often turn out to mean 'yes'."
"I know," said the youth mournfully. "But this one didn't say 'no'. She said, "Aw, phooey!"

* *

Actor: "Yes, my friend, usually my audiences are glued to their seats."
Friend: "What a quaint way of keeping them there!"

* *

Lincoln had more than one altercation with the imperious but reluctant warrior, General McClellan. At one time Lincoln demanded more information from McClellan than he was getting. McClellan, offended, replied with the following telegram:
"We have just captured six cows. What shall we do with them?   G.B. McClellan."

When Napoleon was waging his successful campaign in Poland, several captured Russian officers of high rank were brought before him. Their arrogance to one they considered of low birth made them deprecate all things. "French fight only for gain."
"True," replied their conqueror, "each fights for what he does not possess."

* *

Have you heard about the lady who daily hit her son with a loaf of bread? One day a regular passerby peeped through the window and seeing the lady hitting him with cake, inquired: "Ran out of bread today?"
"Of course not," replied the woman, "but it's his birthday today."

* *

Explorer (just back from Africa): "I brought back six tigers, two leopards and a potfer."
Friend: "What's a potfer?"
Explorer: "To cook the meat in."

* *

Rev. Jones: "Sheriff, there's a dead mule in front of my house."
Sheriff: "I thought you ministers took care of the dead?"

* *

The traveller hailed the first cab to come into the regional wayside stop. "What is your name?" he asked the driver, trying to be friendly.
"Abraham Lincoln, suh," said the man.
"That's a name familar to everybody in this country."
"It oughta be," said the driver. "I been hackin here since right after World War I."

91

Talking about the efficiency of Indian police a business executive narrated this story to his friend:

"Once I'd forgotten my parker pen in the office. When I reached home I thought I'd lost it on the way and accordingly I rang up the police station and got the case registered there. Next day, having found my pen on the office table, I reported the fact to the police station. I was, however, informed by the police authorities that they had already arrested five criminals two of which had also confessed to the theft."

* *

A human being is a guy who'll laugh over a family album, then look in a mirror and never crack a smile.

* *

ETERNAL is for ever and may be even longer.

* *

Briggs: "When are you going on your vacation?"
Higgs: "I don't know. I've got to wait until the neigbours get through using my suitcase."

* *

Some people find their work so fascinating they can sit for hours looking at it.

* *

A secret is something you tell only to one person at a time.

* *

When the warden wished to celebrate his 20th year in the prison, he asked a group of convicts what kind of a party they would like.

Without hesitation they chorused: "Open house!"

·Why are you crying? What's happened?" a mother asked her little son. In between his sobs he replied: "Daddy was driving a nail in the wall and he hit his thumb with the hammer."
"That's nothing to cry about, you silly. Why didn't you laugh?" asked his mother.
"I did," the boy replied.

* *

This one woman of ill-repute refuses to admit married men to her house. Her motto is "I cater to the needy—not the greedy."

* *

"I just got a dog for my wife", one husband told the other.
"I'd like to make a swap like that myself."

* *

Cashier to thief: "My friend take the cashbook also. I'm short of two thousand rupees."

* *

"Do you think long hair makes a man look intellectual?"
"Not when his wife finds it on his coat. It then makes him look foolish."

* *

There is not much difference in the outlook of greying elders and growing youngsters at the seaside. The former admire the beauty of the beach, the latter the beauties.

George Bernard Shaw had a running feud with Churchill. He sent the Prime Minister a note saying, "I am reserving two tickets for you for my premiere. Come and bring a friend—if you have one."

Churchill replied immediately, "Impossible to be present for the first performance. Will attend second—if there is one."

* *

Churchill was always fighting to get more and more protection for England—just to make sure. He used to accentuate his demands with the story of "the man whose mother-in-law had died in Brazil and when asked how the remains should be disposed of replied, 'Embalm-cremate-bury. Take no chances.'"

* *

When the fat woman got on the bus, she called out, "Isn't anybody going to offer me a seat?"

One little fellow got up and said, "I'm willing to make a contribution—anybody else?"

* *

A woman and her son were passengers on a bus and when the conductor asked for their fares, she asked for a half-ticket for the boy. "But he's too old for a half-ticket," the conductor said. "He must be about sixteen, he certainly looks it."

"Well," replied the woman, "can I help it if he worries?"

* *

"What are the differences between psychologists, psychoanalysts and psychiatrists?"

"Psychologists build castles in the air, psychoanalysts live in them and psychiatrists collect the rent."

94

A Frenchman having spent a considerable time in the U.S., was asked what he felt was the most striking difference between the Americans and the French.

"The real difference is perhaps in the fall of the year. The American is sad that the days are getting shorter, while the Frenchman is happy that the nights are growing longer."

* *

"Why does it take three of you guys to file these few papers?" asked the record-keeper.

"Well," retorted the assistant, "Jimmy holds the file, while Frank punches the papers as I put them in the file."

* *

Two young men were discussing the usual subject: girls. "I'm looking for a girl," said one, "who does not drink, smoke or have any bad habits."

"And when you find her," asked the other guy, "what in hell are you going to do with her?"

* *

"I am sorry to hear that your factory was burnt down. What did you manufacture?"

"Fire-extinguishers."

* *

Convict No 600: "It took me nearly two years to complete this book."

Convict No 601: "Oh, that's nothing. It took me five years to complete a sentence."

One friend: How did you become; o successful all
of a sudden?"
Other friend: "Through a strong will."
"What do you mean by a strong will?"
"A will which left me eighty thousand rupees."

* *

And then there was a boss who fired his new secretary for lack of experience. All she knew was
shorthand and typing...

* *

"Why did the foreman fire you?"
"Well, the foreman is the man who stands around
and watches others work."
"Yes, but why did he fire you?"
"He got jealous of me. A lot of fellows thought I
was the foreman!"

* *

Friend: "How are things at your nudist colony?"
Opportunist: "Well, pretty good. I opened up a
little store out there. I sell underthings to the
nudists."
Friend. "What kind of underthings could you sell
to nudists?"
Opportunist: "Cushions."

* *

A fond mother, whose daughter had not come
home at the usual time, grew worried at her abse-
nce. So she telegraphed five of her daughter's
friends, asking where Mary was. Shortly after
her daughter's return, the answers to her telegrams
arrived. Each one read: "Don't worry. Mary is
staying with me tonight."

Instead of feeling sorry for yourself, try feeling sorry for the folk who have to work withy ou.

* *

When you reach 70, you eat better, sleep sounder, feel more alive than when you were 30. Obviously it's healthier to have women on your mind than on your knees!

* *

"You ladies ought to sit a little closer," said the bus conductor in the bus. "According to the Act, every passenger is entitled to 18 inches of seating space." "Sorry," replied the matron, "but we're not constructed according to the Act."

* *

Stop praising a woman and she thinks you don't love her any more. Keep it up and she will think she is too good for you. Come home from work on time and she thinks no else could have you. Come home late and she will say someone else already did.

* *

Two flies were having a conversation on the top of a bald man's head.
"What programme does this remind you of?" asked one.
"I don't know," said the other.
"No hiding-place!" said the first as the man flicked them off.

* *

Two small boys were wandering around the medical college. One hem saw a skeleton on view and said to his friend: "But you don't know what a skeleton is."
"Of course I do," said the other. "It's bones with the people off."

97

A flustered man rushed up to the ticket office and puffed: "I want a ticket to the end of your line on the fastest train!"

"Our fast train just pulled out," he was told.

"Then," gasped the man, "just give me a ticket and point out the track. The moneylender's after me!"

* *

A writer on foreign affairs thinks that "a formula for world peace will be found by someone, sometime, somewhere." Some hope!

Go/Gear
i.e. Game and Gadget

"What do you think about women's fashions of today?"

"Women's fashions are going back to 600 BC—Before Clothing."

* *

It was the first time that the man had ever tried to ride a horse. He nervously pointed this out to the groom at the Riding School.

"Don't you worry about it, Sir," said the groom. "I'm giving you a horse which has never been ridden before."

The policeman stopped a car for speeding. The fair driver explained that she had just washed the car and had to drive fast to get it dry.

* *

Mama Mosquito: "If you children behave yourself, I promise to take all of you to a nudist camp tonight."

* *

"Have you got another razor?" asked the man in the chair of his barber.
"Why?" asked the barber.
"Well, I'd like to defend myself if I can," came the reply.

* *

One way to make the sparks fly is to take a wife with an electric coffee percolator, a husband with an electric razor, a son with an electric guitar, and a daughter with an electric hair drier and put them all together in a house with one socket!

* *

Several men in the smoking-room were arguing as to who was the greatest inventor. One contended for Stephenson, who invented the railroad; another for Edison; another for Marconi; still another for the Wright Brothers.
Finally, one of them turned to a small man, who had been listening but who had said nothing. "What do you think, Mr. Mann?"
"Well", came the reply with a knowing smile, "the man who invented interest was nobody's fool."

A big-game hunter, on safari, disappeared from camp. After a few days, his friends concluded that something he disagreed with had eaten him.

** **

"How come the right side of your car is painted green and the left side is painted yellow?"
"In the event of any accident and if it comes up in court you should hear the witnesses contradict each other!"

** **

"The barber told me a very interesting story as he shaved me."
"Indeed?"
"And he also illustrated it with cuts."

** **

Harry Truman, talking politics with a group of Yale students, was asked by one earnest youth: "How do I start in politics, Sir?"
Replied the former President: "You've already started. You are spending somebody else's money. aren't you?"

** **

"Ever tempted to sell cheap motorcars?" asked the cheerful one.
"The temptation is strong enough," replied Mr. Chuggins. "But there are too many points involved. You know I mortgaged my house in order to buy the machine."
"Yes?"
"Well, I mortgaged the machine in order to build a garage and now I've had to mortage the garage in order to buy gasoline."

An old lady handed the post office clerk a package containing a Bible.

"Anything breakable in this?" he asked.

"Nothing but the Ten Commandments," the old lady replied.

* *

"I have invented a computer that's almost human."

"You mean, it can think?"

"No. But, when it makes a mistake, it can put the blame on another computer."

* *

A gushing young lady embarrassed Edison at a reception by her outspoken admiration. "You will go down in history, Mr. Edison, as the inventor of the first talking machine," she repeated for the tenth time.

"Indeed, no, madam," replied Edison, "I am not the pioneer in the field. The first talking machine was invented by the Almighty and I merely invented one that could be stopped at will."

* *

It's hard to settle down when you return from a holiday—and even harder to settle up.

* *

Facing Ray Lindwall at his fastest in 1948, Johnny Wardle's bat was shaking in his hands as he took guard. "What do you want?" asked Umpire Frank Chester.

"A slow full toss outside the leg-stump!"

One of the running jokes in the days of US President Lyndon Johnson's administration was the President's diet. Mrs. Johnson did everything she could to keep him on it, and he often went to great lengths to indulge himself in his favourite high-calorie treats.

One day, at a baseball game, someone in the large party in the President's box ordered hot dogs and began passing them around. The President was suddenly seen doubled over, his head between his knees, wolfing down a hot dog. Off his diet again, he was afraid that his wife might be watching the game on television and see him eating it.

* *

In a small town, a cricket match was being played. The ball had rapped the batsman in the abdomen region, yet he was given out.
"How out?" he asked the umpire.
"Look in the papers tomorrow!" replied the umpire.
"You look!" said the batsman, "I'm the Editor!"

* *

It was my first trip to the races, and I found the crowds and excitement at the course overwhelming. Firmly entrenched, I made my selections, giving them to my companion to place along with his bets. Neither of us was doing very well until the fifth race, when I won a 20-to-1 long shot. Excitedly, I insisted on collecting the winnings myself while my friend guarded our seats.

Unsure of where to cash in the ticket, I approached a gruff looking old man intently studying the racing form. I asked him, "Can you please tell me which line is for winning tickets?" To which he replied without looking up, "The shortest one, lady!"

Arthur Schnabel, the world-famous pianist, used to charge £5 for each piano lesson, even in 1930.
"I do give lessons at £3," he once admitted, "but I don't recommend them."

* *

A 1913 car-owner's manual states: "The automobile has now developed to the point where it is not anticipated there will be further developments or changes, and this manual should be a reliable guide for the motorist of the future."

* *

Comedian Joey Adams took care of a ringside heckler by saying, "Do you mind if I have you X-rayed? I want to find out what people see in you."

* *

Gerald Goodman, the pop harpist, was asked how he'd managed to be asked to play at Carnegie Hall. He responded, "By pulling strings."

* *

With the frequent melees and the dust kicked up by the horses, spectators found it difficult to follow the details of a polo match at the Bangalore parade grounds. The commentator, however did his best, mentioning the moves and the players as they came into action. The name most frequently heard was that of General P.P. Kumaramangalam, former Chief of the Army Staff.

During a brief interval, I overheard a specatator ask his neighbour how he was enjoying the game. "All I can make out is that two generals seem to be conducting military manoeuvres somewhere out there on the field," he replied. "There's a General Kumaramangalam on one side and genera lconfusion on he other."

He (making the time-worn excuse): "I'm afraid we'll have to stop here; the engine's getting pretty warm."
She: "You men are such hypocrites; you always say the engine."

* *

The Italian government is installing a clock in the leaning tower of Pisa. Reason? What good is it if you have the inclination and you don't have the time?

* *

A well-known snob and show-off was showing friends his new piano, and went out of his way to point out that the keys were made of real ivory. One sceptical friend asked why they were so yellowed and discoloured.
"Oh," replied the snob, "the elephant was a heavy smoker."

* *

Wallie: "Gee, Pop, there's a man at the circus who jumps on a horse's back, slips underneath, catches hold of its tail and finishes up on the horse's neck!"
Dad: "That's easy. I did all that the first time I ever rode a horse."

* *

"I packed my parachute myself," said the nervous student pilot, "but I'm sure it won't open."
"In my opinion," replied the instructor, "you are jumping to a hasty conclusion."

* *

"My grandfather plays the piano by ear."
"Well, if we must boast—my grandfather fiddles with his beard."

Car owner: "I've had this car a whole year and haven't paid a cent for repair or upkeep since I bought it."

Friend: "So the man at the service station was telling me."

* *

"I dreamed last night that I had invented a new type of breakfast food and was sampling it when——"

"Yes, yes; go on."

"I woke up and found a corner of the mattress gone!"

* *

"This is the British Broadcasting Corporation—the next programme comes to you from the Bathroom at Pump; pardon me, I mean the Pumproom in Bath."

* *

The trouble with being a good sport is you have to lose in order to prove it.

* *

"I want a new suit made," the customer said, "and I want it in a hurry."

The tailor shrugged. "I can make it for you," he said, "but it'll take me forty days."

"Oh hell! Why, the Lord created Heaven and Earth in only six days!"

"Sure," said the tailor quietly. "And have you taken a look at it lately?"

* *

Board members to employee: "We're declaring war on inflation, Farnsworth... and you're the ammunition."

106

"Did you hear the one about the bridge expert being the father of twins?"
"Yeah, looks like his wife doubled his bid."

* *

"So your husband refused to buy you a car?"
"He didn't exactly refuse. He said he thought I ought to become more familiar with machinery in general before I started driving. So he bought a washing machine to start on."

* *

"What's happened to your speedometer?"
"I didn't need it, so I took it out and sold it."
"Didn't need it? How can you manage without it?"
"Easy, at 20 mph the exhaust rattles, at 30 mph the door rattles, and at 40 mph I rattle."

* *

Driving instructor: "Now madam, this is the gear lever; down there is the clutch on the left; next to it, in the middle, is the brake; and next to that, on the right, is the accelerator."
Lady: "Just a minute! Let's take one thing at a time. Teach me to drive first."

* *

"You're getting a new car? But the one you had was a swell job."
"It's a whim of my wife's."
"Why don't you put your foot down?"
"Not with my wife. She has a whim of iron."

When Professor Albert Einstein's wife once visited the Wilson Observatory, California, she was shown the gigantic 100-inch telescope with all its elaborate equipment. After marvelling at it, she asked: "What is it used for?" They told her that one of the main purposes was to find out the shape of the universe.

"Oh," said Mrs. Einstein, "my husband does that on the back of an envelope."

* *

A man stopped at a small town garage and told the mechanic, "Whenever I hit eighty, there's a terrible knocking in the engine."

The mechanic gave the vehicle a prolonged and thorough examination, and after much testing, wiped the grease from his hands and drawled, "I don't see nothing wrong, mister. It must be the good Lord a-warning you."

* *

A certain Mr. Jones had just become the proud father of triplets and straightaway he wrote a letter to the secretary of his local club announcing the great news. The secretary of the club mentioned the matter to several members and they got together and presented Mr. Jones with a large silver cup.

Mr. Jones was extremely pleased with the cup and promptly sat down and wrote out a grateful acknowledgement which ended as follows: "Is this cup mine outright or do I have to win it three times?"

And here is this interesting story heard against Lord Hislop:

"A truck driver had collided with him and when asked why he hadn't the sense to drive round his Lordship, replied: "I had the sense, sir but I hadn't the petrol."

* *

The General Manager of a British bank was transferred from London to Paris and the Branch Manager at London had arranged a dinner at his residence in honour of the General Manager. Before the dinner was arranged at the table, the Branch Manager suggested a game of golf. The General Manager lost both—the game and his temper and shouted angrily at his subordinate: "Do you do anything else in the office besides playing golf?"

* *

Driver: "I'm sorry, sir, the car won't move further, there is no petrol in it."
Car owner: "It's perfectly alright. Drive back to the office!"

* *

Golfer: "Boy, how many did I take to do that hole?"
Caddy: "I'm sorry, sir, I only went to a primary school."

* *

Husband (down at three no-trump doubled): "You might have known I didn't have a heart, partner."
Wife (sweetly): "Oh, to be sure. But I did think you had a brain, darling."

"Look here," said the irritated chess wizard, "you've been watching over my shoulder for three hours. Why don't you try playing a match yourself?"

"Aw," drawled the kibitzer, "I ain't got the patience."

* *

The couple drove in from the mountains for their first look at a genuine fourteen-carat circus. Liza saw a zebra for the first time. "Hank," she said, "what kind of animal is that there?"

Hank was stumped. He hadn't seen one before either. "Why, Liza," he said authoritatively, "that's a sports model jackass."

* *

Passer-by: "You're digging out the holes, are you Mr. Halloran?"

Gardener: "No, mum. Oi'm diggin' out the dirt an' leaving the holes."

* *

Director: "So you say you can end all unemployment."

Candidate: "Yes sir."

Director: "How had you planned to do that?"

Candidate: "Well, I'd put all the men on one island and all the women on another."

Director: "And what would they be doing then ?"

Candidate: "Building boats."

* *

An air warden said: "Halt" as a car approached a checkpost. The car halted and the driver put his head out. "What do you want me to do?"

"My orders are to say 'Halt' three times and then shoot. Run away before I have said, 'Halt' twice again."

"Do you think that television is an improvement over radio?"

"Surely! Because all nonsense you speak, you can now see it on television!"

* *

As he was fiddling with the radio dial, he felt a sudden sharp pain in his back. "I think I'm getting lumbago," he cried. "Why bother to listen?" asked his wife, "you won't be able to understand a word of it."

* *

Two writers rented a house for a year and got a promise from the landlord to redecorate the place. When it became obvious that he wouldn't keep his promise, the writers had their attorney draw up a paper giving them permission to decorate the house at their own expense. The landlord was happy to sign.

Two days before they moved out, they had the whole place painted black.

* *

The little boxer had unexpected luck and had just defeated a bigger man. When congratulated, he began to boast and ended up by saying that he could defeat anybody. His opponent, who was still smarting under the defeat, thereupon brought in a friend of his, an enormous heavyweight. "Can you defeat him?" he asked.

"Sure I can." drawled his conqueror and then, after a significant pause, added: "At billiards!"

On my way to work one morning, a man pulled out from the kerb directly in front of my car and dented my front bumper. We both got out of our cars and exchanged identifications.

Upon getting my fender repaired, I forwarded the bill to him. I received the following reply: "Enclosed is a cheque for the amount requested. Hope it has not caused you too much trouble. It's always a pleasure to touch fenders with a lovely lady."

* *

An Irishma gician made a feature of sawing a woman in half. After his retirement a friend asked him what had happened to his assistant. "She's living now in Belfast and Dublin," he answered.

* *

"Come out and play," shouted a little girl in front of her friend's house.

"I can't," called her friend from the window. "If I don't watch Dad, he won't do my homework."

* *

"Did the new play you saw yesterday have a happy ending?"

"Yes. Everybody was glad when it was over!"

* *

"Charlie says he's going to have biggar wheels fitted to his mini-car."

"Why?"

"Dogs keep wetting the windows."

The announcement flashed on the cinema screen. "Will the owner of car number SFR 3968492711 MT please go outside? The car is all right, but the number-plate is blocking the car-park exit."

* *

At the water cooler : "They gave him a watch when he retired, and in a week it stopped working too."

* *

"How did you enjoy the bridge party last night?"
"It was just fine till the cops came and looked under the bridge."

* *

A provincial hardware firm made a special display of household labour-saving devices. In their window was exhibited a large notice stating: "Don't kill your wife with hard work. Let us do it for you."

* *

When the family buys a new car:
Father's question: "How many miles to a gallon?"
Mother's question: "What colour is the upholstery?"
Daughter's question: "Has it a good mirror?"
Son's question: "How fast will she go?"
Neighbour's question: "Where the blazes did they get the money?"

* *

In the business world, an executive knows something about everything, a technician knows everything about something—and the telephone operator knows everything.

"Yes, I came face to face with a lion once. To make matters worse, I was alone and weaponless."

"Goodness! What did you do?"

"What could I do? First I tried looking straight into his eyeballs, but he kept crawling up on me. Then I thought of plunging my arm down his throat, grabbing him by the tail and turning him inside out, but I decided it would be too dangerous. Yet, he kept creeping upon me. I had to think fast."

"How did you get away?"

"I just left him and passed on to the other cages."

* *

A young man-about-town took a glamorous girl out one night. They were driving down a moonlit country lane when the engine suddenly coughed and the car came to a halt. "That's funny," said the young man. "I wonder what that knocking was?"

"Well, I can tell you one thing for sure," the girl answered icily. "It wasn't opportunity."

* *

A pretty young woman entered a music shop and went to the counter where a new clerk was sorting out sheet music. "Pardon me," she said, "but have you 'Kiss Me in the Park One Night?' "

The clerk looked at her, startled, and blushed. "S... sorry, Miss," he stammered, "but it must've been the clerk at the other counter. I've only been here a week."

* *

What part of the car causes the most accidents?
The nut that holds the wheel.

One reason that dances at nudist colonies are so popular, we've been told, is that the girls can see what they're up against.

* *

Whenever an armed forces pilot is involved in an aircraft accident, he has to make a statement about the cause. One young pilot summed up his mishap thus: "I believe the cause of the accident was administrative, I should never have graduated from a flying school."

* *

The present extensive use of cosmetics merely proves that women are making up for lost time.

* *

Female voice to bus driver: "Can't you wait until I get my clothes on?"
Fifty soldiers twisted their necks out of joint while the laundress climbed aboard with a basket of clothes.

* *

One girl said: "I like men who make things. Like Tom made 300,000 rupees last year."

* *

Travelling behind a small delivery van one morning, I read its company slogan: "Experts in all types of fastening." Then I noticed that the van's rear doors were tied together with a piece of string.

* *

Mrs. Fozzle (to bridge expert): "In the same circumstance, how would you have played the hand?"
Bridge expert: "Under an assumed name, madam."

"I turned the way I signalled," said the lady driver, indignantly, after the smash.
"I know it," retorted the man. "That's what fooled me!"

* *

"How is the car you bought?"
"The only part of it that doesn't make a noise is the horn."

* *

A young man had a brother and a girl-friend who had birthdays on the same day. He naturally bought each of them a present. For his brother he bought a shotgun and for his girl-friend a bottle of expensive perfume. For his girl-friend he wrote a note which said: "Use this on yourself while thinking of me." She got the right note but the wrong present!

* *

A husband and wife approached one of those penny scales. He jumped on the scale and put in a coin. "Listen to this fortune," he said enthusiastically to his wife as she peered over his shoulders:
"You are bright, resourceful and energetic and will go on to be a great success."
"Yeah," said the wife. "And it's got your weight wrong, too."

* *

Warning to young ladies: "If you wear loose clothing, beware of the machinery. If you wear tight clothing, then beware of the machinist."

Grandpa was doing some carpentry at home and asked his grandson to bring him a screwdriver. The kid came back a few minutes later and announced, "I have the vodka, but I can't find an orange."

* *

The conductor, making his rounds on the train, was surprised to find a little old man rolled up under one of the seats. Caught in his hideout, the little man pleaded: "I'm a poor old man and haven't got the money for a ticket. But my daughter is being married in another town and I simply must get there for the wedding. Please let me stay here. I promise to be very quiet and not disturb any of the passengers."
The conductor was a kindly man and agreed. But, under the very next seat, he found another little old gent huddled up and looking badly frightened.
"And where are you going?" he asked.
The man answered: "I'm the bridegroom!"

* *

Arriving a little before half-time at a football match, a young lady asked the score and was told "No goals."
"Thank God for that!" she said, "I haven't missed anything."

* *

A police officer stopped a car which was zigzagging alarmingly and asked the driver what he was doing.
"I'm learning to drive," was the reply.
"What? without an instructor?" exclaimed the officer.
"Oh yes," answered the driver. "It's a correspondence course."

An elderly gentleman was fascinated by all the instruments in the cockpit. He asked the pilot. "How did you get along before you had those electronic gadgets?"

"Very simple," was the reply. "I'd land somewhere and ask the stewardess to go out and buy a coffee cake. Then I'd look at the address of the bakery on the cake box and find out exactly where we were."

* *

Speaking of the satisfaction he had enjoyed in being an orchestra conductor, Leonard Bernstein observed: "It's a remarkably lucky thing to be able to storm your way through a Beethoven symphony. Think of the amount of rage you can get out. If you exhibited that on the street or in an inter-personal relationship, you'd be thrown in jail. Instead, your're applauded for it."

* *

Not long ago the construction company for which I work took on some additional workers. They had never done any carpentry before, and one of them just couldn't catch on. In exasperation, the head of the work crew told him, "Son, we often have people who don't know what's going on around here. But I'm afraid you don't even suspect anything."

Hog/Heal
i.e. Hotel and Hospital

Customer: "What's this fly doing in my soup?"
Waiter: "Swimming!"

* *

After 25 years' service, the proof-reader had trouble with his eyesight, so he retired and opened a diner.
"Look here," yelled a customer. "There are needles in my soup."
"Typographical error," said the proprietor.
"It should have been noodles."

A customer sat at a table in a smart restaurant and tied his napkin round his neck. "Try to tell him as diplomatically as possible," the manager said to the waiter, "that it's not done here."

The waiter paused thoughtfully, then said: "Pardon me, Sir, shave or haircut?"

* *

The woman visiting her husband in hospital took the pretty young nurse aside. "Tell me the truth," she said "Is he making any progress?"

"Absolutely none!" the nurse replied. "He's just not my type!"

* *

"You have a very clean restaurant," remarked the patron to the owner. "Thank you," replied the owner. "And what in particular prompts you to say so?"

"Everything tastes like soap."

* *

A teenage boy was admitted to hospital with appendicitis. Just before his operation, the nurses were puzzled when they heard the boy's mother ask the surgeon if there was a barber in this hospital. "Why do you want to know?" they asked.

"I thought," she replied, "that we could get his hair cut while he's under the anaesthetic."

* *

When a rich man was in the hospital he had a day nurse and a night nurse. In the afternoon he rested.

Customer: "Waiter, hurry, I'm late already! Will the pancakes be long?"

Waiter: "No sir, they'll be round."

* *

Rani had a fit of coughing, just when a telephone call came for her.

The operator apologised: "I'm sorry, Rani can't speak to you now She's having a coughing break."

* *

It is considered improper and discourteous to walk out on your host before the party ends. Wait and be carried out with the rest.

* *

"Waiter, what's wrong with these eggs?" asked the customer.

"I don't know. I only laid the table."

* *

The sweet young thing signalled a taxicab and said to the driver: "To the maternity hospital and never mind about rushing—I only work there!"

* *

"How do you treat sleeplessness?"

"I strike at the original cause of the trouble."

"Here's the hammer, Doc. Only, don't strike the baby too hard!"

* *

Customer: "There's a piece of soap in this plate."

Waiter: "That's all right—it's to wash down the food!"

"Where are you going, boy?"
"I'm going down to get myself some tuberculosis stamps."
"What are they? I haven't heard of them."
"Every year I get myself fifty cents worth of tuberculosis stamps and stick them on my chest and I haven't had tuberculosis yet."

* *

The management of a hotel received a notice from the police, reading: "Please keep your back door locked to prevent theft," and another from the fire department, reading: "Please keep your back door unlocked to facilitate exit in case of fire."
The management held a meeting, and decided to have two doors, one to be kept locked, and the other open.

* *

As a Hungarian refugee during the Second World War, I had to spend a few days in a military hospital in Gloucestershire, and I asked for permission to use my typewriter. The ward sister, a kind, middle-aged spinster who had never before come across a British soldier with an accent like mine, listened to my request, thought for a while, then said: "All right, you can have your typewriter, but on one condition: you must give me your word of honour that you won't do any subversive work on it."

Bernard Shaw had been invited to dinner at an expensive restaurant where everything was posh but the service was too slow for his liking. His host, who was very proud of the occasion and had spared no expense in selecting the menu, was commenting on each course as it was served. When the snails came, he said: "Snails are a speciality of this place."

"So I see, but why disguise them as waiters?" quipped Shaw.

* *

Consultant: "If I considered an operation necessary, would you have the money to pay for it?"

Private patient: "Let's put it another way, Doc. If I didn't have the money to pay for it, would you consider the operation necessary?"

* *

Casualty officer: "How on earth did you manage to break both your legs?"

Patient: "Pure habit. I threw my cigarette down a manhole and stepped on it!"

* *

At the bottom of the menu of an Indian restaurant in London is the following message: "Service charge of ten per cent is added. Please leave no gratitude."

* *

Some of the best bedtime stories can be found in hotel registers.

The beggar approached an old maid for a slice of bread. "But why," said the old maid, "should a strong man like you be found begging."

"Dear lady," replied the beggar, "it's the only profession I know in which a man can approach a beautiful woman without an introduction."
He got a full loaf.

* *

Wife to clergyman eyeing waiter at restaurant: "Let him snicker. If you want angel cake, order angel cake."

* *

A friend confessed to me why she was now taking a serious interest in dieting. It seems that recently her husband had asked her, ' Do you realize there are 15 kilos of you that I'm not legally married to?"

* *

The harried stockbroker suffering from insomnia never got to sleep before dawn, then slept right through the alarm and so never made it to the office in time. Upon being reprimanded by his boss, he decided to consult the doctor. The doctor gave him some sleeping-pills and that night he fell asleep immediately and experienced a pleasant rest. In the morning, he woke up before the alarm rang, jumped out of bed with new verve and vigour. When he arrived at his office promptly, he told his boss: "Those pills I got from my doctor really work! I had no trouble at all waking up this morning."

"That's nice." the boss replied, "but where were you yesterday?"

There had been severe floods in the valley and the Health Officer hurried to the scene. He queried one old couple: "The water supply may be polluted. What measures are you taking here?"

The old chap assured: "First we boil the water. Then we filter it. Then, for safety's sake, we drink beer."

* *

Dina had been having trouble with an ulcerated tooth for some time before she got up enough courage to go to a dentist. The moment he touched her tooth she screamed murder.

"Why are you making so much noise?" demanded the doctor. "Don't you know that I am a painless dentist?"

"Well, sir," retorted Dina, "maybe you are painless, but I am not."

* *

Policeman (in restaurant): "Your car awaits without."

Diner: "Without what?"

Policeman: "Without lights. Name and address, please."

* *

"A steamroller ran over, my uncle," said one.

"What did you do?" asked the other.

"I just took him home and slipped him under the door."

* *

HOSPITAL: Where a nurse wakes you up to give you a sleeping pill.

The patient was a beautiful young showgirl who complained of nervous tensions. The doctor prescribed a programme of tranquillising pills and told her to come back in a couple of weeks and let him know how she felt.

When she returned, the doctor asked her if she felt different and she replied: "No, doctor, but I've noticed that other people seem a lot more relaxed!"

* *

A worried father hurried to his teenage son's hospital bedside. The lad had a broken leg and many cuts and bruises. "What happened, son?" asked the father. "Did you have an accident coming home from your girl's house?"

"No," the boy groaned.

"Well, how did it happen?" persisted the father.

"We were jitterbugging," the boy explained, "when her old man came in. He's deaf and couldn't hear the music—so he threw me out of the window."

* *

The young waitress went to the Head Waiter and said, "I'm not going to serve that cheeky devil over there."

"Why not?"

"Well, he asked me for French salad and when I said 'What's that?' he said, 'It's the same as any other salad, only you serve it without dressing.'"

* *

She: "I'm afraid I can't afford that operation now."

He: "No. It looks like you'll have to talk about your old one for another year."

A waiter explained about tipping in restaurants: "Ten per cent of your bill—that's a tip. But 20 per cent—ah, 20 per cent is a gratuity!"

* *

Hack: "I'm so sore from running that I can't stand or sit."
Mack: "If you're telling the truth, you're lying."

* *

"You must come to my housewarming next Friday."
"Fine! I'll bring the matches!"

* *

"It seems they had to give Mrs. Brownsmith ether twice for one operation."
"How come?"
"Once to perform the operation and once to keep her from talking about it."

* *

Guest: "And the flies are certainly thick around here."
Hotel manager; "Thick? What can you expect for two dollars a day? Educated ones?"

* *

Lady: "Can you give me a room and bath?"
Clerk: "I can give you a room, madam, but you will have to take your own bath."

* *

Irate guest: "Look here, the rain is simply pouring through the roof of my bedroom."
Summer hotel proprietor: "Absolutely according to our prospectus, sir. Running water in every room."

Visitor to a Hotel Clerk (in a coal-mining city).
"This wall is so thin that you can almost see through
it."
Manager: "That's the window you're looking at."

* *

Customer: "Say, sister, take this coffee away. It's
like mud."
Waitress: "Well, it was ground just this morning."

* *

"Waiter, we want chicken. The younger the better."
"Then hadn't you better order eggs, sir?"

* *

Customer: "Where is that turtle soup I ordered?"
Waiter: "I'm sorry, sir, but you know how turtles
are."

* *

"I can't eat this garbage," cried the enraged diner.
"Call the manager."
"It's no use," said the waiter. "He won't eat it
either."

* *

"Waiter, bring me a ham sandwich."
"With pleasure."
"Nope, with mustard."

* *

Customer: "Waiter, waiter, quick, there is a hair in
my soup."
Waiter (sleuthing): "Blonde or red? We're missing
a waitress."

Mrs. Harris (who misread the clinical thermometer): "Doctor! you had better come at once. My husband's temperature is 120!"

Doctor (calmly): "My dear Mrs. Harris, if that is so, it's too late for me. You should call the fire department."

* *

A student nurse was representing her ward in an inter-hospital quiz. In the general knowledge round, her question was about the Statue of Liberty. "In one hand she holds a tablet," said the question master. "What is in her other hand?"

Hazarded the nurse, "A glass of water?"

* *

In the smoking-room of the big hotel, the Scot had been boring everyone with tales of the great deeds he had performed.

"Well, now," said the Englishman at last, "suppose you tell us something you can't do? By Jove, I'll undertake to do it myself!"

"Thank you," said the Scot. "I can't pay my bill here."

* *

Mama: "Eat your spinach, dear; it makes strong teeth."

Johnny: "Why don't you feed it to Grandpa."

* *

Dad (to his bright son): "What's wrong?"

Son: "I had a terrible scene with your wife."

Fields had finished his meals, and when the waiter brought the bill, he smiled and said: "Well, I am sorry, but I just haven't got any money to pay the bill."

"Oh, it's all right," said the waiter. "We'll just write your name on the wall, and you can pay the next time you come in."

"Hey, don't do that," Mr. Fields protested. "Everybody who drops in will come to know about it."

"No, nobody would," said the waiter. "We are going to take off your overcoat and hang over it."

* *

Getting down from the stairs of the hotel, the young boy tried his best to talk to the beautiful lady who was coming down next to him. But in vain. Finally when they both came down, the boy said bitterly: "Pardon me, I thought you were my mother."

The beautiful lady smiled sweetly at him. "I couldn't be," she replied. "I'm married."

* *

Lately two French tourists arrived in India and went to see Kashmir. They got a room in a beautiful hotel. To their surprise, they were attacked by mosquitoes, an insect new to them.

They turned off the light and crawled under their bedsheets. One of them just peeped to see if the insects had gone. "It's no use," he groaned, seeing some glow-worms that had flown into the room, "come out, they've come with lanterns looking for us."

Customer: "For this hopeless food you're billing five dollars?"

Hotel Manager: "Shut up! This comes to you through the courtesy of Almighty God."

* *

This appeared outside a restaurant in America: "We prepare our tea out of best Asian tobacco."

* *

Richard entered a popular restaurant one night and ordered roasted chicken. After the usual waiting time, it arrived; Richard took one look at it and complained to the waiter, "The chicken is certainly burnt black."

"Yes sir!" said the waiter. "A mark of respect, sir. Our head cook died yesterday, sir."

* *

The customer, who was having a look at the menu of one of the popular city restaurants, enquired: "What's the difference between the yellow-plate special and the white-plate special?"

"The white-plate special is one rupee extra."

"Is the food any better?"

"No, but we wash these plates."

* *

Customer: "How is the food here?"

Waitress: "I'm a waitress here, not a witness!"

* *

Patron: "I don't like all the flies in here."

Waiter: "Point out the ones you don't like, sir, I'll evict them."

On a late arrival at a party being given in a prominent Paris restaurant, a man asked for something tall, cool and full of gin.

"Let me introduce my wife," urged the host.

* *

Hotel manager: "Here are some views of the hotel for you to take with."

Departing customer: "Thanks, but after eating your food for three days, sleeping on one of your beds, and seeing what you have charged, I have my own views of your hotel."

* *

Hotel manager: "Did, you enjoy the cocktail party?"

Young lady: "Enjoyed it! One more drink and I'd have been under the host!"

* *

Stevenson: "My friend Lord is dying, and I can't get his prescriptions anywhere."

James: "Why, one chemist is open day and night even on Sundays."

Stevenson: "Yes, but it is a dry day."

* *

"This is the seventeenth operating table you've ruined this month, Doctor. Please don't cut so deep."

* *

"Doctor, come quickly. My wife has swallowed a fountain pen."

"I'll be right over! What are you doing in the meantime?"

. Using a pencil."

"For God's sake, man," said the dentist to his patient, "stop making those noises and waving your arms in front of you. I haven't even touched your tooth yet."

"I know," said the patient desperately. "But you're standing on my corn."

* *

George had undergone an operation of his eyes. As soon as he recovered consciousness, he discovered that all the shades in his room were drawn. The next moment he found the doctor coming in. He gathered strength and courageously asked the reason for the drawn shades.

"There's a fire across the street," the doctor said. "I pulled down the shades because I didn't want you to think the operation had been a failure."

* *

The patient was getting his eyes tested. The optician brought a card for his reading. And he read the figure "Twelve."

"Young fellow," said the optician, "you need glasses rather badly. I've just shown you a picture of film stars."

* *

"Hey, doctor, look my Jimmy has swallowed the matches."

"Here, use my lighter."

* *

Patient : "How much for an eye operation?"
Doctor : "£100 in advance."
Patient : "Why in advance?"
Doctor : "Because I am going to operate upon you and I may not succeed."

Mrs. Smith was in hospital for the last two weeks and Mr. Smith had come to see her.

"Don't worry, darling. You're going to be all right. I just figured it out. We owe the doctor—rupees five hundred for the operation, the anaesthetist—rupees one hundred and the X-Ray clinic—rupees seven hundred. Believe me, darling, with all we owe them—they can't afford to let you die!"

* *

The ambulance brought the young lady to the hospital in bad shape. She was scratched and was bleeding, her clothes were all torn. She was rushed into Emergency and the surgeon examined her wounds.

"What happened ?" the doctor asked. "Were you run down by a drunken driver ?"

"No," she answered weakly, "I was picked up by one."

* *

Interviewing a new nurse, the Superintendent of the Hospital asked why she had left her last post.

"I didn't like the set up," said the nurse frankly. "The child was backward, and the father was forward."

* *

Nurse : "It's twins, madam !"

Patient : "Nonsense ! I never had a date with two persons."

* *

Doctor : "Nurse, what happened to the patient who was on bed 272 ?"

Nurse : "She was running a fever of 105, so I put her with the guy who has the chills."

134

Waiter to diner: "Do we honour credit cards? Sir, we venerate them."

* *

As a salesman, I frequently stopped in a small New Zealand town where I stayed at a hotel known for appalling service. On my first visit I made the mistake of ordering tea in bed. Shortly before seven, a girl threw open the door. "Sugar in your tea?" she shouted. "No, thank you," I replied. As she banged the door shut, she said. "Ah, well, don't stir , then."

* *

"I hear your sister is sick in bed, Bobby," remarked a neighbour. "Nothing serious, I hope?"

"Not specially," answered Bobby. "We were just playin' a game, seeing who could lean the furthest out of the window, and she won."

* *

Hostess: "Won't you have something more, Tommy?"

Tommy: "No thank you, I'm full."

Hostess: "Well, then, put some fruit and cakes in your pockets to eat on the way home."

Tommy: "No, thank you, they're full, too."

* *

Joe: "I'm tired. I was out with a nurse last night."

Jack: "Cheer up. Maybe your mother will let you go out without one some time."

The pretty restaurant cashier had applied for a vacation.

"I must recuperate," she said, "my beauty is beginning to fade."

"What makes you think so?" asked the proprietor.

"The men are beginning to count their change."

* *

"I have brought you a Red Cross nurse," announced the doctor.

"Take her back," said the peevish patient, "and get me one that's blonde and cheerful."

* *

Hospital visitor: "Your wife misses you quite a lot, I am sure."

Bandaged patient: "Oh no, she is a good shot. That's why I am here."

* *

Patient: "I'm in love with you. I don't want to get well."

Nurse: "You won't. The doctor saw you kissing me and he's in love with me, too."

* *

Clerk: "Sorry, madam, but Mr. Gotcash has just gone to lunch with his wife."

Mrs. Gotcash: "Oh! Well, then tell him his stenographer called."

* *

A doctor was telling his friend that he loved a woman who was visiting his consulting room regularly.

"Why don't you marry her?" enquired the friend.

"I can't afford it," replied the doctor. "She is my best patient."

Lately Carry had arthritis-twinges in her hinges. "It took a lot of will-power," she bragged, "but I've finally given up trying to give up smoking! I am so full of penicillin," she continued, "If I sneeze I'll cure someone!"

* *

At the lunch counter: "Do you think if I have onion with my hamburger I'll get heartburn?"

"For 75 cents you get a hamburger; three dollars is the charge for medical advice."

* *

Wife (to husband returning from the doctor): "Well did the doctor find out what you had?"

Husband: "Almost. I had twenty-two dollars and he charged me twenty."

* *

A visitor to the insane asylum asked the attendant how they decided when a patient was well enough to be sent home.

"Well," said the attendant, "the doctors are too overworked to check all the patients, so we turn on the faucet that supplies that big trough over there, We leave the water running and tell the patients to take buckets and empty all the water out of the trough."

"How does that show anything?" said the visitor.

"Well, a patient who is cured will merely turn the faucet off."

"Well, I declare," marvelled the visitor. "I never would have thought of that."

* *

Chickens are the most useful animals. You can eat them before and after they are born.

137

Folks who take cold baths never have rheumatism
...but they have cold baths.

* *

He suffers from eyestrain. He lives opposite the
Y.W.C.A.

* *

A Scotsman, an Irishman, a Frenchman and an
American were eating dinner together.
When the meal was finished and the waiter came
with the bill, the Scotsman promptly said he would
take it.
The next day an American ventriloquist was found
murdered.

* *

TOURIST RESORT is a place where no one knows
how unimportant you are at home.

* *

X-RAY is a machine used mainly to illustrate the
letter X.

* *

POST-MORTEM is when they send a dead corpse
through the post office.

* *

ORPHANAGE is a home for dead parents.

* *

At a dinner party, a Congressman was asked: "What
do you consider the object of legislation?"
"The greatest good of the greatest number," replied
the Congressman.
"And," continued the questioner, "what do you
consider the greatest number?"
"Number One," replied the Congressman.

President Lincoln was once stricken with what proved to be a mild form of smallpox. Of course no one dared enter the White House for fear of contagion, and Mr. Lincoln remarked: "Is it not too sad, that now, while I have something to give to everybody, no one comes near me!"

* *

The goat was in the dumps and picked up a can of film. After he ate it all up, his friend asked him, "How was it?"

"To tell the truth," he answered, "the book was better."

Love/Let
i.e. Love and Life

True musician: When one hears a lady singing in the bath, he puts his ear to the keyhole.

* *

The dignified old businessman decided to spend a holiday in a small town. So his secretary sent word to the local hotel-keeper, asking him to arrange "a well-furnished room, special food, etc. etc." Arriving in the town, the tycoon was shown the best room in the hotel. After he had expressed satisfaction, he was led to an adjoining room where two comely lasses waited. "And who are these young ladies?" he asked.

"The two et ceteras," replied the hotel-keeper.

Said the professor's wife: "George, do you know what day it is? Twenty-five years ago today, we first became engaged."

The absent-minded professor looked shocked. "Twenty-five years! why didn't you say so before? It's high time we got married!"

* *

"I love your daughter very dearly, sir," said the young man. "I would suffer deeply if I ever caused her a moment's unhappiness."

"You certainly would," replied the father. "That girl is her mother all over—and I should know!"

* *

First soldier: "What made you go into the army?"
Second soldier: "I had no wife and I loved war, so I went. What about you?"
First soldier: "Well, I had a wife and loved peace, so I went."

* *

Baptiste Matte and his wife, Elena, of Ecuador, as good Catholics, disapproved of divorce. So when Baptiste took a mistress eight years ago, Elena turned a blind eye—and found herself a lover. For convenience, both mistress and lover lived in the Mattes' home in Quito—for a while. Then Baptiste found another mistress who found solace with Elena's lover. So Elena found a replacement. Now all six live happily together.

Which would you rather be in—an explosion or a collision?" asked a soldier.

"In a collision," replied the soldier.

"Why?"

"Because, in a collision, there you are; but, in an explosion, where are you?"

* *

When discussing their wedding plans, **Canadian** grocer Steven Ling told his bride, Jasmine Henson, that he wanted to invite to the ceremony a few **pen** pals with whom he had been communicating, " Okay," she said, "you invite them. It'll be **all** right with Mum and Dad." But it wasn't. When 263 pen-pals arrived from various parts of Canada and the United States. many expecting accommodation for a few days, Jasmine's parents asked the police to keep the hordes from their home near Victoria, British Columbia. The couple quarrelled— and cancelled the ceremony.

* *

Patient: "It's a painful thing to mention, but my wife thinks the fee you charged for my operation was far too high."

Surgeon: "But, my dear sir, surely you do not set the same low value on your life as your wife does?"

* *

Thoreau once observed that, if he knew for certain that a man was on his way to see him with the single purpose of trying to help him, he would run for his life.

* *

The surest sign that a man is in love is when he divorces his wife.